儂心所慕兮　牧羊在何許
亭午歇何方　曷不發一語

שִׁיר הַשִּׁירִים

雅 歌

THE SONG OF SONGS

Ἆσμα Ἀσμάτων

Canticum Canticorum

漢譯者 王福民

插畫者朱一雄　編校者丁　星

文史哲出版社
The Liberal Arts Press

雅歌 / 王福民漢譯. 歌底斯英譯. -- 初版. --
臺北市，民82
面；　公分
ISBN 957-547-790-1(平裝)

241.39

雅歌

英譯者：歌底斯
漢譯者：王福民
插畫者：朱一星
編校者：丁　雄
出版者：文史哲出版社
登記證字號：行政院新聞局局版臺業字五三三七號
發行所：文史哲出版社
發行人：彭正雄
印刷者：文史哲出版社
台北市羅斯福路一段七十二巷四號
郵撥○五一二八八一二彭正雄帳戶
電話：三五一一○二八
中華民國八十二年六月台一版
實價新台幣二二○元

目　　錄

ACKNOWLEDGEMENT

1. To Doctor Robert Gordis, professor of the Jewish Theological Seminary of America, for his kind permission to reprint the full text of his translation of the SONG OF SONGS, copyrighted 1954.

2. To Doctor Charles C. Dold, assistant to the Executive Secretary, Division of Christian Education, National Council of the Churches of Christ in the U.S.A., for granting the permission to reprint the Scripture text of the SONG OF SONGS from the Revised Standard Version of the Bible, copyrighted 1946 and 1952.

3. To Mr. I-Hsiung Ju, for the colorful illustrations he made for this book.

Ong Hok Ben

吳經熊博士對語文雙譯
雅歌的評價

福民先生道鑒：

　　昨日收到尊譯「雅歌」一冊。今晨開始拜讀，不忍釋卷，實命世之譯作也。其中白話及五古兩體，各有優長。先誦白話，後吟五古，尤覺有味。

　　古人云「下筆若有神」，足下有焉。

　　序言知此書之成，乃從千辛萬苦中產生，更證吾人一切成就，莫非吾主十架之花之實。

　　序中謂結縭纔將兼旬，即辭家作客，此為人間最苦痛事，目前諒已團圓，心焉祝之！弟於前年十一月卅日喪耦，至今猶依依也。曾口占一絕云：「洞房花燭宛如昨，四十四春夢一場。最是臨終辭別意，與君相會在天堂。」末句乃記其告別之言也。

尊譯附錄，見道之語也。而第三節中說「入我母親的家」之精義尤獲我心。弟在羅馬時，日記中有下列一則：

O my Jesus, once you were incarnated,
*　　now I beg you to be incarnated again.*
Be a Chinese, amongst the Chinese.
In my mother's house, be you my brother,
*　　nursed at the breasts of my mother.*
Be you naturalized in my mother's house,
*　　that my mother's house may be super-*
*　　naturalized in the House of your Father.*

June 28, 1947

　　觀此可見吾二人同受聖神之靈感，同氣相求，同聲相應，豈不然乎？雅歌為弟平素所愛讀，今得足下精心之漢譯，更覺有意矣！

匆復順頌

道安

　　　　　　　　　　　　　　弟吳經熊頓

　　　　　　　　　　　　　　一九六一年二月十四日

JOHN C, H. WU
3 REYNOLDS PLACE
NEWARK 6, NEW JERSEY

福民先生道鑒。昨日始到

尊譯雅歌一冊。今晨開始拜讀、

不意譯卷實命世之譯作也。其

中白話及五古兩體各有優長。先

誦白話、次吟五古、尤覺有味。古人

云「不華葉而召神」。豈不有焉。觀

序言知此書之成、乃淬千年萬善中產

JOHN C. H. WU
3 REYNOLDS PLACE
NEWARK 6, NEW JERSEY

先天証吾人一切成就、莫忘此吾主十字架

之花之実、序中語偶禍瀟洒重

句、即解家必家生為人間家普

痛來月莫涼之團圓心為祝

文！承杆前年十百曾春耦差

娟依々也。曾口舌一絕云:「洞房

花燭哀如作。四十四春夢一場景

JOHN C. H. WU
3 REYNOLDS PLACE
NEWARK 6, NEW JERSEY

是時將辭別去、「與君相會在天
堂。」末句乃記其告別之言也。
考譯州報、見遠之語也。而第三節
申說、「不負母親的家」、措辭尤
獲我心。予幼喪母時、日記中已不引一節

JOHN C. H. WU
3 REYNOLDS PLACE
NEWARK 5, NEW JERSEY

觀士弓兄与二人同鑒 聖神之霝

感，同氣相求同聲相應，豈不

益乎雅歌乃弟平素所愛讀

令譯 益不彫心之澤澤更覺

至意 毋庸順頌

道安

弟 吳經熊

一九六二年首
之〇日

序言

廿年前於明燈道聲合刊上見吳譯
聖詠第十九首詞藻淵雅道意深湛
心竊慕焉曾試譯詩篇廿三首爲五
古登閩南聖會報戊子夏六月結縭
綰將薰旬即辭家作客珉水湄僦居
轆打牢某公寓早則入市上課亭午
之後蟄處寓中幽憂無俚有怨美訴
泪乎祖國局勢急轉直下骨肉至親

夢寐時縈晨興沐橫之餘唯經言是念風簷展讀籍慰旅懷殘臘向盡立顏據英文姆士王聖經迻譯雅歌為五古越歲孟春甫載而成四篇於信心生活故而二豎蠢動不違寧慶且誤信醫言頻死者屢幸蒙　主恩使得復起麻後奔走衣食日無暇暑前惰未續倏逾十年矣戊戌仲夏摯友丁星先生由牛津歸來每共晨夕輒以竟其全功為勸今春於課隙強成其五六兩篇四月上旬假期開始酷暑中揮汗捉躯薰人以赴中旬未薙草方具又本英文標準新譯加以惰訂月秒初稿乃完先是丁子代向細約猶太教神學院求得歌底斯莫

說論氷之至，婦德之頌，聖掩也，盡同列世情，刻畫
文同列世情，而郁抉万世情。

其導人倫之翕，其新二節宗基眷之夫，聖而無所閒。夫文濟而郁，抉万世情。

寫人蓋籍以悅其（賽章六五二節）佳耦，如得雅歌中之聖，而無盡夫病意淋漓而郁勃，近風繡口。

撰料事，聖經每之念，曲亦奮春意近風繡口。

白話詩廿九首撰寫導論。

成廣搜資料，始行嚴事，故聖經郎每是也。

以送迨三，滿始男女亞尔然，當斯為人之至於矯揉營卐，尤膽作家繡口。

依復見唯以悅尔良人然，被譽其描摹聖傷生境造千古作家繡口。

為猶其愛其佳白歌中之性愛之至，香旺春味近作家之繡口。

更擊復始姑先知之曰，教會歌以其況體，蓋若傷此歌而造千古關。

譯明輪大道，上帝保羅愛雅歌者飾宮，未樂府過之關。

（章五五節廿五）

3

侶之蕙心雜誦之者如入伊甸如登蓮島誠詩國獨闢之勝境教會奧秘之妙廓也丁兹末造著此微言寧起斯民扵頑溺澆薄俗之浮覽使推其區區之愛暢其涓涓之流以放乎四海而會其有極耶夫陶鎔經史行遠言文之道也驅會中西闢蹊涉曠之方也蛻變之新文學有待綆汲猶太靈源而浚發東傳之基督教必因勤宣聖經妙諦而繁榮余不敏弗敢以言此唯欲就正時賢藉知固陋激敷有道敢拋整甄廢幾歌中之歌宏揚正聲扵六合聖中之聖照灼紫氣扵千秋頌而頹也

主曆一九五九年九月一日
扵菲京彙簫讀書室

凡　例

一、本書的五古漢譯根據標準英文新譯（ Revised　Standard
　　Version ）， 白話漢譯根據美國紐約猶太教神學院出版的
　　歌底斯（ Dr. Robert　Gordis ）英譯 The　Song　of　Songs，
　　並且徵得他們的同意，取這兩部英譯做對照。

二、本書的導論是根據歌底斯的成說和 Interpreter's Bible的導
　　論撰寫而成的；且取同時期中國的一些詩歌作參證；可說
　　是一篇比較文學史。這兩種漢譯的譯法，實受導論的論點
　　所左右；所以希望讀者先看導論，然後誦讀譯作；先讀導
　　論，然後批評譯作。

三、五古譯作採用意譯，白話譯作採用直譯。為使意義圓滿，
　　白話譯作有幾個地方增添了一些字，並效法官話漢譯，在
　　增添的字旁加點，以資識別。

四、因為許多詞題已在導論裏詳細論列過，且白話譯文每段均
　　有說明，所以沒有「註釋」；如讀者認為有需要，請卽賜
　　示，以便再版時增添。

五、附錄了一篇講稿，讓讀者看到雅歌對屬靈事工的啓示的一
　　種例子。

1

羚羊深山歇　母鹿郊外行
勿令落荒躓　勿使夢中驚
郎儂方繾綣　欲飽飫春情

導 論

一 解題

A 至上的書

雅歌直譯是「歌中之歌」(The Song of Songs)。這樣的名稱在以色列人眼中是超特的，無比的。比方舊約時代的會幕及聖殿，被稱爲聖所，裏面有個至聖所，由大祭司按規矩抽籤，輪流每年一次進到裏面去燒香。至聖所直譯是「聖中之聖」(Holy of Holies)。以色列人頌揚上主，稱他爲「萬王之王」，「萬主之主」(The King of Kings, The Lord of Lords)。這些都有至高 (Most High)，無倫 (Uniqueness) 的意思。

阿基巴拉比 (Rabbi Akiba) 說過一句很有分量的話：「整個宇宙是沒有價值的，直到雅歌賜給以色列人之日；因爲全部聖經都是神聖的，而雅歌是聖中之聖」(Robert Gordis: The Song of Songs p.1)。這話會叫人駭異，因雅歌表面上看來毫

1

無宗教色彩或民族色彩的，竟被高舉到這樣的程度。

在集中找不到上帝的名號，在八章六節裏「耶和華的熱焰」，標準英譯本作"A most vehement flame"據Interpreter's Bible 註釋：這是希伯來人用以代表具有至高力量的神聖名號（ Volume 5，144 ）。至於具有國家主義色彩的「錫安」，只在第三章第十一節裏提到一次。

阿基巴拉比的那句話，據我的猜想有兩種意義，第一，這歌集以男女之愛以況喻上帝和以色列民族之愛：「少年人怎樣娶處女，你的衆民也要照樣娶你；新郎怎樣喜悅新婦，你的上帝也要照樣喜悅你。」（ 賽62:5 ）。以親子之愛況喻耶和華和選民之愛。八章雅歌裏提到「我母親」四次（ 1:6,3:4,8 1,8:2 ），「懷我者」一次（ 3:4 ），「他母親」一次（ 3:11 ），「她母親」一次（ 6:9 ），「生養她者」一次（ 6:9 ），「你母親」一次（ 8:5 ），「生養你者」一次（ 8:5 ）。次數雖不多，所表現的情感，却很濃厚。「婦人焉能忘記她吃奶的嬰孩，不憐恤她所生的兒子；卽或有忘記的，我却不忘記你。看哪，我將你銘刻在我掌上，你的牆垣常在我眼前」（賽49:15 、16 ）。先知的說法是以色列人精神的反映，而雅歌被認爲以隱喻的方式出之，所以更加要眇，更加優美，而能感人至深，收效較先知的戟指痛斥爲大。第二，雅歌是一部很優美的文學作品，和普通的經典不同；沒有雅歌，整部聖經便失却「溫柔敦厚」之旨。

是的，男女之愛是人生最大的奧祕，當上帝創造男人亞當，使他住在伊甸園裏之後，覺得他獨居是不好的，便叫他沈

睡，取了他的肋骨，造了一個女人，領她到他跟前。亞當說：「這是我骨中的骨，肉中的肉，"This is bone of my bones, and flesh of my flesh"」 （創2:23）。

有「骨中的骨，肉中的肉」的微妙關係，才能唱出「歌中之歌」，冒出「耶和華（萬王之王，萬主之主）的無上熱焰」來。

雅歌自公元九十年Jamnia會議重新確定它為聖經中不可或缺之一卷後，地位從沒有搖動過。

B 思無邪

雅歌是「歌中之歌」，和中國的詩經一樣是世界第一流的文學典籍。孔子批評詩經說：「詩三百，一言以蔽之，思無邪」。許多人如果真明瞭詩經的內容，一想到十五國的國風，定會懷疑孔子的說法；特別是有道學家那種方巾氣的人。朱熹在他的詩經註譯裏常以「淫奔之辭」為題解。既然詩經的國風裏充滿了「淫奔之辭」，何以孔子竟說它是「思無邪」？原來站在道學家狹隘的立場來看，的確國風裏充滿了「淫奔之辭」；但若站在文學、藝術的立場來說，國風的確是「思無邪」。站在道學家的立場是要表彰「善」，站在文學藝術的立場是要表彰「美」。歸根究柢，「善」和「美」是二而一，一而二的。儒家注重人倫。人倫沒有男女的關係是建立不起來的。俗語說：

天下事從一室始

世人情由平旦初

道家注重順乎自然。如果抹殺男女的關係便是違反自然；墨

3

家主張兼愛 ；如果不着重男女之愛， 在邏輯上也講不過去。
法家雖然慘礉寡恩，但如漠視男女的關係，也無從施法令，申
刑禁。

詩經國風第一首關睢中有：

窈窕淑女　　寤寐求之
求之不得　　寤寐思服
悠哉悠哉　　輾轉反側

這幾行，譯爲語體是：

美貌賢淑的女子

我在夢中尋求她

尋求却求不到

我睡在床上想念她

愁思像悠悠的水流

叫我翻來覆去睡不著

這樣的內容，詩序竟說它可以「風天下而正夫婦」。

儒家解釋關睢，都根據孔子的「樂而不淫， 哀而不傷」
（論語八佾）而立論。荀子和史遷都有「國風好色而不淫」的
說法，就是告訴我們美感和快感有分別。國風所給人家的是美
感，而不是快感；現代一些沒有價值的小說或電影，給人家的
是肉感與快感，而不是美感。

歌底斯拉比（Robert Gordis）在其所著雅歌的序文裏說：

The inclusion of the Song of Songs in the Biblical ca-
non is evidence of the persistence in Judaism of the basic
conception that the natural is holy, being the manifesta-

4

tion of the Divine. On this score too, the Song of Songs,
to borrow Akiba's phrase, is the Holy of Holies.

（ —The Song of Songs，P. 10 ）

茲逐譯如下：

雅歌被收入聖經裏，證明猶太教所堅持的基本概念卽人性是聖善的，由於它是從神性中表現出來的。基此：可引用阿基巴拉比的名言：「歌中之歌是聖中之聖」。

上帝本自己的形相以造人；上帝吹氣給人，使他成爲有靈的活人；上帝是靈，拜他的要用心靈與誠實；這些是猶太教和基督教對人性的基本認識。人的一切旣出自上帝，上帝特賦給他有超越其他動物的品質（和上帝同樣的），使他能夠認識上帝，和上帝交契，並宰制萬物；那麼，人性的聖善，是無容置疑了。

雅歌用高度的文學手法以表現人類至性之愛的優美，高尙，樂趣，尊嚴，神聖，且被認以人類至性之愛而況喩神人之愛，當然是「歌中之歌」，「聖中之聖」了。

說雅歌是「歌中之歌」，「聖中之聖」，和孔子說詩經是「思無邪」，眞可算是異曲同工了。

不過荀子和史遷所說的「國風好色而不淫」，乃強調美感是高尙的，肉感是卑汚的。雅歌的描寫人類至性之愛却是大胆的，把美感和肉感交融爲一的。

中國幾千年來詩歌的基本概念是以詩經爲張本：「國風好色而不淫，小雅怨誹而不亂」。杜甫詩歌理論的中心是「別裁僞體親風雅」。裁汰僞體，不悖詩經好色不淫，怨誹不亂的原

5

則，以風雅為飯。但西洋人却大胆地以藝術模擬人類的性慾，以文學描繪人類的性慾，雅歌可說是其泉源之一。

在詩經的國風裏雖然充滿了男女愛情的篇什，但大胆地描繪性慾的却未曾見；勉強去搜索僅有「周南」的「野有死麢」：

野有死麢　　白茅包之
有女懷春　　吉士誘之

・　　　　・　　　　・

林有樸嫩　　野有死鹿
白茅純束　　有女如玉

・　　　　・　　　　・

舒而脫脫兮　　無感我帨兮
無使尨也吠

語譯如下：

野地裏有死獐
用白色茅草包裹
有個女子在懷春
有個情郎在挑逗

・　　　　・　　　　・

樹林裏有小木
野地裏有死鹿
用白色茅草包束
有個女子莊麗得像美玉

・　　　　・　　　　・

要慢慢地來啊

6

別動我的門帘啊

別惹起狗吠啊

「野有死麕」這一首，解釋者言人人殊。顧頡剛氏曾解釋末段的「舒而脫脫兮，無感我帨兮」，說是女郎感到性慾的滿足而顫抖，胡適之先生說是太過了（古史辨第三册詩經之部）。有人把「帨」字解作蔽膝之巾。那麼，「無感我帨兮」，便反映那吉士在動手動脚了。其實這是一首很美麗的描寫戀情的發生與幽會的情景的詩。用白茅包着死麕以形容女郎雖有莊重的外表，却有懷春的內心。死麕包着白茅，看起來很潔白，不久那腥臊的味道終要透出來的。女子被吉士的挑逗，一天不表露春情，兩三天終會表露的。最後一段描寫那吉士跑去和那靜女幽會，那靜女溫存地說：「要慢慢來啊！」斥責地說：「別動我的門帘啊！」終又警戒地說：「別惹起狗吠啊！」把靜女初次和吉士幽會的患得患失，半推半就的神情完全表露出來。所以這首詩也合乎「好色不淫」的條件。

雅歌却不然。它三次描繪男女床笫的私事（2:6，7；3:5；8 4）茲舉二章六至七節作證：

O that his left hand

　　Were under my head,

　　　And that his right hand embraced me!

　　　·　　　　·　　　　·

I adjure you, O daughters of Jerusalem,

　　By the gazelles

　　　or the hinds of the field,

7

That you stir not up nor awaken love

Until it please.

我的五古譯文如下：

　　　左手爲儂枕　　　右抱背至襟

　　　　　·　　　　　·　　　　　·

　　　郇城衆女分　　　諦聽余叮嚀

　　　羚羊深山歇　　　母鹿郊外行

　　　毋令落荒躚　　　毋使夢中驚

　　　郎儂方繾綣　　　欲飽飫春情

C　所羅門之歌

　　雅歌的標題：「所羅門之歌，歌中之雅歌」；英文作：
"The Song of Songs, which is Solomon's."。關於 The Song
of Songs（歌中之歌），我們在前面已經詳細申論過了，現在
來討論「所羅門之歌」。

　　雅歌是一部戀愛詩的集粹（The Song of Songs is an ant-
hology of love poems．見 Gordis: The Song of Songs p.18)。
那麼：雅歌裏面七次提到所羅門要怎樣解釋呢？

　　在第一章第一節裏的標題讓許多後人相信雅歌就是所羅門
的作品。列王紀上 4:30-31 記着：所羅門的智慧超過東方人，
和埃及人的一切智慧，他的名聲傳揚在四圍的列國。他作箴言
三千句：詩歌一千零五首。

　　在這裏又好像得了一個佐證：「他的詩歌有一千零五首。」
猶太的拉比們認爲「所羅門寫過三部經典：箴言，傳道，和雅
歌。那一部是先寫的？……大拉比海耶（Hiyya）說：所羅門

8

先寫箴言，其次雅歌，再次傳道書……約拿丹拉比（Jonathan）說：他先寫雅歌，其次箴言，再次是傳道。約拿丹拉比是根據人性之常而言的。一個人在年青時代，他唱情歌；當他一切都成熟了，就實踐箴言；當他年紀老了，就看破萬事，而作傳道書。」（本節譯自 Gordis: Th· Song of Songs 第九面）。

但據歌底斯拉比集合學人研究的結果：「所羅門之歌，歌中之雅歌」這標題是編纂這歌集的人所加的，非原來的式樣（參閱原書第十八面）。

第一章第五節裏「所羅門的帳幕」，這正像後代人所說的「所羅門王的寶藏」（King S lomon's mine），「路易十四的家器」（Louis XIV furniture）一樣，和所羅門沒有什麼直接的關係。

第八章十一，十二節裏，所羅門是用以代表一個擁有鉅額財富的代表，好像「煤油大王」或「百萬富翁」之類。

在第三章裏還有三次提到所羅門（7、9，11）這些支持了傳統的說法：所羅門卽雅歌中的「良人」（參閱列王紀上十一：1），或稱作「王」。此論看來有理，實則不然。 在三章七節中的所羅門沒有加上「王」字；而雅歌中其他許多地方用「王」字（一：4，12；七：5）卻不飾作所羅門。所以全書就是這一段提到所羅門是比較特別的。

這一段（三：6至11）曾被多數人認爲農村結婚進行曲。但詳細研究一下，有以下的困難：

1，這段裏有「煙柱」（六節），「六十個善戰的勇士」（七節），和普通詩歌的誇飾不同。十節中有「純銀作柱，黃

金作底，坐墊紫色，裏面鋪着象牙」，這決不是想像的。鄉曲的愛侶可以在山林中彼此對說：「我們用香柏作屋棟，絲杉作屋椽」（一：17），但在有限制的情景中提到喬皇華麗的轎車，絕不是質樸的農人們所能歌唱得出的。

2，「耶路撒冷衆女子」（3：10）這詞語在雅歌中多次提出（一：5；二：7；三：5；五：8，16；八：4），但「錫安的衆女子」（三：11）只在這裏提過一次，別的地方再看不到。巴勒斯坦的特徵瀰漫全書，而具有民族色彩的標誌——以色列，只在這裏出現一次（三：7）。

3，所羅門的名在這裏無法刪掉。第七節沒有「王」字，而所羅門卻不可或缺；十一節如削去「所羅門」字樣，就破壞了詩歌的韻律（指原文）。

這一段無論如何不是農村的結婚歌，因為它的場面豪華，又具有民族意識的色彩。所以這一段被假定為描寫所羅門和外國公主結婚的歌曲，那公主可能是埃及的。

這首詩可作如此解釋：那公主由埃及地上來，有很多的扈從，在曠野中安營，有點像漢妾王昭君出塞的情形；他們在野地燃起煙火。公主的轎車是所羅門送去的，周遭有六十個以色列的勇士保護着。那轎車是用名貴的香柏木為骨榦，是所羅門和腓尼基人通商而輸入的。其裝飾依所羅門奢侈的習性有純銀，黃金，深紫色的坐墊，是耶路撒冷貴族婦女所製成的。

這首詩和詩篇第四十五首記載以色列王和一個腓尼基公主結婚的性質相似。詩篇四十五首是向王和公主歌頌的，而雅歌的這一段是敍述埃及公主從曠野裏上來的情形，較像國風裏召

10

南的「何彼襛矣」：

　　何彼襛矣　　唐棣之華
　　曷不肅雝　　王姬之車
　　·　　　　·　　　　·

　　何彼襛矣　　華若桃李
　　平王之孫　　齊侯之子
　　·　　　　·　　　　·

　　其釣維何　　維絲伊緡
　　齊侯之子　　平王之孫

兹試譯成白話詩：

　　怎會那麼襛艷
　　活像唐棣之華？
　　怎不叫人肅然起敬
　　王姬的轎車！
　　·　　　　·　　　　·

　　怎會那麼襛艷
　　活像春天的桃李？
　　是平王的外孫
　　齊侯的愛女
　　·　　　　·　　　　·

　　她怎樣地垂釣？
　　用絲線和細繩
　　是齊侯的愛女
　　平王的外孫

11

這場面當然不及所羅門的了！

二　時地

A　詩歌與歷史

雅歌是純粹的抒情詩，看不出有什麼歷史的背景，大部份的詩篇都無法繫以年日。

如果講起以色列人的歷史興趣，可以說是勝過印度人。印度人在佛書上常有「距佛出生十萬劫」之類的記載，簡直是在說神話。以色列人的經典，大部份是史籍，記年月也相當清楚，如摩西五經中的利未記，民數記，申命記等；至列王紀，歷代志的史筆已相當謹嚴。當然這些仍比不上中國的典籍那麼準確。中國在兩千五百年前就有一部編年史的春秋；每一史事，繫以年月，絲毫不苟。其後史遷，班固等的成就更加偉大。原來中國人是最富歷史興趣的。

中國的詩，據聞一多的說法，就是記事的歷史。

「詩」字最初在古人的觀念中，却離現在觀念太遠了。漢朝人每訓詩為志：

詩之為言志也（詩譜序疏引春秋說題辭）。

詩之言志也（洪範五行傳鄭注）。

詩，志也（呂氏春秋慎大覽高注，楚辭悲囘風王注，說文）。

……志有三個意義：一記憶，二記錄，三懷抱，這三個意義正代表詩的發展途徑上的三個主要階段（聞一多全集甲一八五）。

12

謝无量也說：

詩與歷史，最有關係。周代采詩，本用史官。
詩就是一種史料。文中子上有一段：「子謂薛收曰：
昔聖人述史三焉。其述書也，帝王之制備矣，故索焉
而皆獲。其述詩也，興廢之由顯矣，故究焉而皆得。
其述春秋也，邪正之述明矣，故考焉而皆當。」（詩
經研究第七十面）

是的，毛詩序也說：「……治世之音安以樂，其政和；
亂世之音怨以怒，其政乖；亡國之音哀以思；其民困。……至
於王道衰，禮義廢，政教失，國異政，家殊俗，而變風變雅作
矣。國史明乎得失之迹，傷人倫之廢，哀刑政之苛，吟詠情性
以風其上，達於事變，而懷其舊俗也。……」

中國古時的詩和歷史息息相關，是大家公認的。

按照詩序的說法，幾乎詩經裏每首詩都可清楚畫出它的歷
史背景，都和當時的歷史人物有關。詩經每首詩都可反映當時
的政治和社會的生活，是不錯的：如果說全是和當時的歷史人
物有關，那未免有點牽強。

詩經的年代始於公元前一千一百五十年間，止於公元前五
百五十年間。公元前一千一百五十年間的詩歌如大雅大明：

<pre>
天監在下   有命既集
文王初載   天作之合
在洽之陽   在渭之涘
  ·   ·   ·
文王嘉止   大邦有子
</pre>

13

大邦有子　　俔天之妹
文定厥祥　　親迎於渭
　　．　　　　　．　　　　　．
造舟作樂　　不顯其光
有命自天　　命此文王
於周於京　　纘女維莘

　　文王之妃太姒，是莘人的女兒，有賢德。這首詩是描寫文王娶她的時候，親迎之於渭濱的情景，和雅歌三章，六至十一節描寫所羅門王迎娶外國公主的情景相似。詩經這首詩側重天命和門第，不像雅歌那一首注重排場的豪華。

　　詩經至吳公子季札聘問列國（公元前五五四），觀周樂時已完成。國風可與史事互證的不勝枚舉，如秦風的黃鳥：

交交黃鳥　　止於桑
誰從穆公　　子車仲行
惟此仲行　　百夫之防
臨其穴　　　喘喘其慄
彼蒼者天　　殲我良人
如可贖兮　　人百其身

是寫秦穆公埋葬時三良殉葬的史事。

　　詩經也有許多詩篇，只能反映當時的社會生活，而無法確指是剌某人或剌某事的；舊說有許多是靠不住的。比如鄭風的「緇衣」，詩序說：「緇衣，美武公也。父子並為周司徒，善於其職，國人宜之，故美其德」。茲錄首節如下：

緇衣之宜兮，

14

敝，予又改爲兮。

適子之館兮，

還，予授子之粲兮！

譯爲新詩：

黑布衣裁製得很合身，

破了我再替你改製。

你上你們的辦公處去，

囘來時我用笑臉迎着你！

這完全是描寫夫婦和悅的生活。妻子在丈夫出門做事之前，對丈夫說的一些溫存的話，絕沒有什麼讚美公侯的迹象，許多解詩的人被成說所蔽。這首詩反映當時社會的安定，人民的知足，所謂「治世之音安以樂」者也。

雅歌中除三章六至十一節可確指是描繪所羅門王用轎車迎娶外國公主而外，其他也都和歷史人物無關，但可反映當時的社會生活。茲舉八章十一至十二節爲例。這段歌底斯的英譯還較標準譯本清楚：

Solomon owned a vineyard at Baal Hamon

Which he gave over to tenants.

For its fruit one would give

A thousand pieces of silver.

But my vineyard, my very own, is before me.

You, Solomon, are welcome to your thousand,

And your vine-tenders to their two hundred!

我五古的譯文如下：

15

請看所羅門	置一葡萄園
交園丁經管	在巴力哈文
爲園中果實	人須付千元
余之葡萄圃	區區此一廛
佳果爲我熟	嬌花亦嫣然
敬陳所羅門	君自獲一千
園丁培壅苦	應得兩百員

這詩的寓意是說：所羅門有他的財富（Baal Hamon 可譯作富豪），有他的后妃；我也有我日光下應享的分：擁抱着荆釵之妻，也有人生的樂趣。

B　雅歌的時代

雅歌的時代，起點比詩經稍遲，在所羅門王卽位之後，乃公元前九百六十年，終止期比詩經早，約在北國以色列淪亡於亞述手中之前（前七百廿二年）。

第三章六至十一節旣被鑒定爲描摹所羅門王和外邦公主結婚的情景，雅歌開始於公元前九百六十年之後是沒有問題的了。第六章第四節拿北方的得撒和南方的耶路撒冷對照，那麼那首詩不能遲於公元前八百七十六年暗利建都於撒瑪利亞之時。暗利在位共十二年，建都在得撒共六年，然後以兩他連得銀子，向撒瑪買了撒瑪利亞山，在山上建城；按着山地原主撒瑪的名，稱他的都城爲撒瑪利亞。事見列王紀上十六章二十四節。

雅歌集中充滿歡樂逸豫的情緒，絕不見有被擄或亡國的蔭影；也沒有古列時代的以斯拉，尼希米重修耶路撒冷及重建聖

16

殿那樣的宗教氣氛與願力。 如果照中國人的說法， 這是「正聲」，而非變風變雅可以比擬。是的，所羅門王是以色列國最強盛的時代，其後國家雖分裂爲二，一切的情景大致不差，是猶太民族、國家的黃金時代，直到公元前七二二年，北國爲亞述所滅時爲止。

「治世之音安以樂，其政和；亂世之音怨以怒，其政乖；亡國之音哀以思，其民困」（詩序）。雅歌集中沒有衞風的「氓」那「怨以怒」的聲調：

　　……女也不爽　　士貳其行

　　　　士也罔極　　二三其德

也沒有王風的「黍離」的「哀以思」：

　　彼黍離離　　彼稷之苗

　　行邁靡靡　　中心搖搖

　　知我者　　謂我心憂

　　不知我者　　謂我何求

　　悠悠蒼天　　此何人哉

C　雅歌的地理背景

希伯來人所居住的迦南地（Canaan）西南越過西乃（Sinai）區及紅海（Red Sea），就可到尼羅河（River Nile）下游的埃及（Egypt）；北部的山地是它和另一文化帶米索不達米亞（Mesopotamia）的過度地帶。它是肥沃新月形地區（Fertile Crescent）的西區，一向和東區的兩河流域（River Euphrates and River Tigris）並稱，也是西方兩大文化發祥地的緩衝區。他們的祖先由米索不達米亞出來，後來下埃及地去，又

和迦南地的土著發生密切的關係，所以學得了巴比倫的法典（Hammorabi），學了埃及人的科學，以及迦南土著的生活方式。

希伯來人在巴勒斯坦（Palestine）建國，僅經三個君王——掃羅（Soul），大衛（David）和所羅門（Solomon），便分裂爲兩國；這段的時間是公元前一零二五至公元前九三五年。全盛時員幅北收亞蘭人（Aram）的領土入版圖，南越西乃區與埃及地相接，及分裂後，北部縮至黑門山地（Mt. Hermen）以南，南部則縮至西乃區以北（請參閱聖經地圖）。

雅歌的時代既經判定是公元前九六零年所羅門王登極後，及被擄至巴比倫（公元前七二二）前的產物，那麼，它的地域就是希伯來人全盛時代的版圖了。

這個地帶沒有尼羅河及幼發拉底河與底格里斯河的定期氾濫，且沒有開展的平原，農業當然不能太過發達，僅北部有幾處肥沃的流域，比較富裕；南部因雨量不足，土地磽瘠，所以這地方是半牧畜和半農業的經濟地帶。雅歌自然也具備這種色彩，多次提到牧人，羊羣，葡萄園。兹舉第二章十六，十七節爲例：

> My beloved s mine and I am his,
>
> He pastures his flocks among the lilies.
>
> Until the day breathes
>
> And the shadows flee,
>
> Turn, my beloved, be like a gazelle,
>
> or a young stag

18

Upon rugged mountains.

這兩節我的五古譯文是這樣的：

良人屬乎我　　我屬我良人
良人牧羊在何許
百合花叢綴綠茵
清風起天際　　煙歛雲翳飛
良人猶牧羊　　遨遊知所歸
嵯峨山上鹿　　蹣跚偎芳菲

詩經和楚辭却到處令我們聞到農業社會土壤溫馨的氣息；
如楚辭離騷中的：

余既滋蘭之九畹兮
又樹蕙之百畝
畦留夷與揭車兮
雜杜衡與芳芷
冀枝葉之峻茂兮
願俟時乎吾將刈

詩經周頌的「思文」：

思文后稷　　克配彼天
立我蒸民　　莫匪爾極
貽我來牟　　帝命率育
無此疆爾界　　陳常于時夏

又「噫嘻」：

噫嘻成王　　既昭假爾
率時農夫　　播厥百穀

駿發爾私　　終三十里
亦服爾耕　　十千維耦

雅歌中的佳人，稱讚她的良人是「好牧人」，在芳菲中牧放；楚辭離騷中屈原自稱爲播種香草名花的園丁；詩經周頌中周人歌頌他們丕顯的祖先是善於發展農業經濟的領袖。

雅歌中的許多城市，山嶺，谷地和鄉土，顯示這部歌集是希伯來王國全盛時代的產物。雅歌的地理背景顯然地以北部以色列爲重要，甚至許多次提到敘利亞（Syria）的地域：在外約但地區，南北邊都曾提到。至於南部的猶大則很少提到。大衞和所羅門二王的版圖正達到雅歌所提北部及約旦河東的這些地帶。

西北部的山地曾提及的是黑門（Hermon）山和示尼珥（Senir）山，又有正北的利巴嫩（Lebanon）山和亞瑪那（Amana）山。在北國以色列的中部有書念城（Shunem）是屬乎加利利（Galilee）境內的，和撒瑪利亞（Samaria）相鄰；腓尼基人（Phoenicians）地界的南端靠海的迦密（Carmel）山；迦密山南部的海岸平原沙崙（Sharon）谷地；書念南部，靠近約旦河的得撒（Tirzah），北國的王者暗利曾在此建都六年，前面已經提過了。外約旦（Transjordan）的地區曾在歌中出現的有南部基列區（Gilead）的希實本（Heshbon），可能還牽連到北部的巴珊（Bashan）。至於猶大國的地域絕少被提及。在三章十一節中提到錫安（Zion），這是具有民族色彩的。數度提及耶路撒冷（1:5; 2:7; 3:5,10; 5:8,16; 6:4; 8:4）；這兩個名字同屬一個地方。此外：只有死海附近的隱基底被提及。

20

從這些地點可得以下的結論：這歌集肇端於所羅門時代，所以活動範圍遠達敍利亞、外約旦地區，終止於北國淪亡在亞述人手中的時候。因爲南部的地區很少被提及，可見是以北部爲活動的中心。

當然了，集中雜有波斯文字，如四章十三節中的 Pardes（Gordis: The Song of Songs p. 23），所以這歌集在波斯時代曾被編纂及潤飾過的，那是在公元前五六世紀之間。

詩經的地理背景是黃河中下游的渭水，涇河，鎬水，澧水，汾河，沁水，淇水，衞河的流域之間；楚辭的地理背景是長江中游的雲夢沼澤地，洞庭湖盆，及其支流湘，資、沅、澧流域之間：是上好的農業地帶；雅歌是產生在約旦河流域之間，是農牧兼半的地帶，因地區的寬狹不同，所以留下來詩篇的數量，也有豐仄的懸殊。

三 性質

A 是祀神曲嗎？

對雅歌的性質最摩登的解釋是認爲它是祀神曲，並且說是希伯來人譯自「外邦」的。聖經上的史籍不絕地記載着選民隨從迦南地的人民敬拜外邦的偶像，所以這歌集就是外邦淫祀的寫照，和中國楚辭九歌中的湘君、湘夫人一樣。一九一四年捷西（Neuschatz de Jassy）發表論文說雅歌是祭祀埃及主神奧賽累斯（Osiris）典禮的歌曲；同時威特肯特（Wittkindt）又說是祭祀巴比倫和亞述所崇拜的宇宙生殖神哀絲塔（Ishtar）用的歌曲。

巴比倫的農業神叫搭模斯（Tammuz）。 相傳他爲其妻哀絲塔所殺。後此神由下界送囘，逐成爲植物在季節中死而復生的表徵。巴比倫人祀爲農業神。猶太人染了拜搭模斯的淫祀的禮俗，聖經多次記載，以西結八：14，15節：

> 他領我到耶和華殿外院朝北的門口，誰知在那裏有婦女坐着，爲搭模斯哭泣。他對我說：「人子啊，你看見了麼？你還要看見比這個更可憎的事。」

因此密克（T. J. Meek）氏在一九二二年發揮偉論說， 雅歌是祭祀搭模斯的歌曲。這說法曾發生極大的影響。

接着莫文克爾（Mowin k l）及其他的學者把這論調擴大到舊約許多典籍上去，認爲裏面有豐富的祀神歌曲，大部份是採自迦南人的宗教信仰的。被指爲這一類典籍的，包括詩篇，何西亞，約珥，哈巴谷，路得記；有的全部是，有的部份是祀神曲。

哈拉（Hall ）宣稱雅歌是祭祀「春之神」哈瑪沙特（Hag Hamazzot）的歌曲， 是選民效法迦南人的結果。 迦南人在這種的祀神曲中的「良人」就是巴力（Baal），那女郎就是亞斯他錄（Ashtoreth或As'arte）。 巴力是腓尼基人和迦南人崇拜的神，是代表男性，日頭，如同希臘神話中的周必特（Jupiter），或九歌中的東皇太一 ； 亞斯他錄是迦南人所崇拜的女神，代表女人，月亮 ， 如同希臘神話中的凡紐斯（Venus）。王上十六章卅二節：

> （尼八）在撒瑪利亞建造巴力的廟，在廟裏爲巴力築壇。

這樣的事不勝枚舉。王上十一章第五節：

> 所羅門隨從西頓人的女神亞斯他錄，和亞捫人可憎的
> 神米勒公。

選民拜亞斯他錄的事也不一而足。所以哈拉會猜定雅歌乃近東祭祀死而復活之神（The dying and reviving god）的歌曲之擴充。

這些主張雅歌是祀神曲，而且是以色列人效法外邦人敬拜偶像時，從外邦得到資料，或模倣他們的淫祀而製成雅歌之說法，實在經不起考驗。根據珥理克（A．B．Ehrlich）氏所說一句評衡聖經性質精警簡潔的話：「聖經是希伯來人用一種宗教為根基的民族文學」（The Bible is the Hebrews' national literature upon a religious foundation）。無疑地，宗教觀念滲透希伯來人生活的每一角；古代以色列人的民族生活完全以宗教為依飯，但人的肉體和人性絕不能受抹煞，特別是智慧文學的境域中，人性的慾求與願望是非常熱烈的。比方詩篇，戰勝仇敵的慾求，箴言因智慧蒙恩的信念，傳道書於嘗過一切屬世滋味之後，感到空虛，冀盼得到解脫的人生，都是非常的親切。雅歌在聖經中正是屬乎這一類（Area of wisdom）。

前面經已說過雅歌是人類至性之愛的流露，絕不見有宗教的成分，怎麼可以和祀神曲等量齊觀呢？更不要說是外邦的祀神曲了！

前面最後提到有人認為雅歌是祭祀死而復活之神（dying and reviving God）的樂章。主是說的人引證當逾越節時聖殿要誦讀雅歌，最早記載這件事是約在六世紀發行的小冊子「律

法師」（Sopherim），離開雅歌編成歌集時至少一千年。這是專用於節期的，歌頌春天的，那節期和「亞筆月的節期」（Festival of Abib)之性質相同，在出埃及記中有許多關於這個節期的記載：

> 亞筆月間的這日，是你們出來的日子。將來耶和華領你們進迦南…那流奶與蜜之地，那時你們要在這月間守這禮。
>
> ——十三：4、5
>
> 你們要守無酵節，照我所吩咐你們的，在亞筆月內所定的日期，喫無酵餅七天。……
>
> ——廿三：十五

然而雅歌全沒有提到春天節日的事，也沒有亞筆月喫除酵餅的任何痕跡，也沒有提任何祭典。如果說是祭祀死而復活之神，何以沒有對死神獻上哭泣，或說及肉身腐化的資料？

提出上面主張的人又臆說或者以色列把外邦祭祀死而復活之神的樂章，改爲祭祀耶和華的樂章。如果這說法對，爲何雅歌中看不見耶和華的聖名呢？

歌底斯拉比對此問題持反對的看法。他說：「雅歌歌頌的是人性之愛，與神事無關，豐富的內容排拒一切寓言性的解釋。全集所表現的都是現世相的，有思愛成病，有素願得償，有愛侶的調情，疏遠與復和。時常指出巴勒斯坦風土的特殊地區，強有力地排除那些主張雅歌的材料曾被用作祀神曲的論調，因祀神曲的要素是有定型的，將是一種擴展和反覆的活動型式」（Gordis: The Song of Songs 第八面）。

又說：「不管頑固的或新穎的寓言性的解釋，總是受雅歌真面目所摧毀。傳統的猶太教和基督教寓言性的解釋是雅歌自有其獨立而迷人的實在性，決非祀神曲所曾具備」（同上）。

勞黎（Rowley）氏說得好：「我們爲我們的益處，願一直地尋求雅歌的隱喻，在一切的經驗中，推想那些事物是屬靈的，但不是說它是爲此目的而寫的，或作者有這樣的意念存在心中」（同上）。

如果把雅歌拿來和眞正的中國祀神曲「九歌」比較，便可發現有顯著的不同。

1，九歌是神話，雅歌所說的是人事。中國人一向被稱爲缺乏宗教思想的國家，其祀神的九歌，却涵蘊着神祕性，而希伯來人的宗教思想，滲透了他們民族生活的每一隅，其經典中的雅歌，却沒有一點是人性所無，可見雅歌不是祀神曲。

2，九歌有祭祀的對象，雅歌找不到這對象的痕跡。據聞一多氏的說法：九歌所迎送的神只有東皇太一，其他九神「不妨和東皇太一同出同進，而參與了被迎送的經驗，甚至可以說，被「饒」給一點那樣的榮耀」（全集甲二六六）。

祭禮旣非爲九神而設，那麼他們到場是幹什麼的？漢郊祀歌已有答案：「合好效歡虞（娛）太一……九歌畢奏斐然殊」（同上）。

依聞一多氏把九歌列表分類，並與詩經比較，其表如下（全集甲二七二）：

神道及其意義					歌辭					
						内容的特徵與情調			外形	
客體	東君雲中君湘君湘夫人大司命小司命山鬼河伯	（自然神）物	助祀	淫祀		雜曲九章	用獨白或對話的形式抒寫悲歡離合的情懷	似風（戀歌）	哀艷	長短句	轉韻
	國殤	鬼	陪祀	小祀	報功		述戰爭壯烈與英勇	似雅（輓歌）	悲壯	七字句	韻
主體	東皇太一	神	正祀	大祀	報德	祭神曲二章 迎神曲送神曲	鋪敍祭禮的儀式和過程	似頌（祭歌）	肅穆	長短句	不轉韻

那麼，很容易看出九歌和雅歌的不同（祀神曲與非祀神曲的分別）了。九歌的對象是鬼神及自然神（物），雅歌完全是人與人之間的事。良人的對象是靜女，靜女的對象是良人。九歌區區十首詩可分爲戀歌、輓歌和祭歌，就像詩經中的風，雅，頌。雅歌依歌底斯的分法共廿九首，全部是戀歌，如詩經中的風。

九歌這部祀神曲每章都有神靈的影子。

吉日兮辰良

穆將愉兮上皇

．．．．．．．．．

靈偃蹇兮姣服

芳菲菲兮滿堂

．．．．．．．．．

——東皇太一

「東皇太一」是主神，歌中第二行便說明目的。最後又提到神靈臨格的情形。

國殤是向殉國英雄（鬼）報功的。最後兩行：

身既死兮神以靈

魂魄毅兮爲鬼雄

九歌中的戀歌和雅歌也不同。

⋯⋯⋯⋯⋯⋯⋯

九嶷繽兮並迎

靈之來兮如雲

捐余袂兮江中

遺余褋兮醴浦

搴汀洲之杜若

將以遺兮遠者

⋯⋯⋯⋯⋯⋯

——湘夫人

若有人兮山之阿

被薜荔兮帶女羅

既含睇兮又宜笑

子慕予兮善窈窕

——山鬼

這是神話色彩非常濃厚的。蘇雪林女士說是「神人戀愛」，實在是不錯的。雅歌却沒有神靈的影子，是人與人之間的純潔愛情。

聞一多說：「⋯⋯這裏我們可以覺察，地域愈南，歌辭的

氣息愈靈活，愈放肆，愈頑艷，直到那極南端的（文學產物）湘君、湘夫人，例如後者的「捐余袂兮江中，遺余褋兮醴浦」二句，那猥褻的含義幾乎令人不堪卒讀了。……」（全集甲二七六）

這證明九歌是淫祀，當男女在一起跳舞祀神的時候，懸擬人神戀愛的情狀，實地表演出來。

雅歌雖然有極放肆，極頑艷的寫法，却是人與人之間的事情，沒有神靈的影子。猶太教和基督教的神學家，都把雅歌中的男女之愛，以況喻上帝和以色列人之愛，或基督和教會之愛。但那是以人與人之間的肉慾之愛以況喻神與人之間的神聖之愛，和九歌懸擬神與人戀愛而由人與人加以表演的不同。九歌中的淫祀，和希臘神話的故事，如周必特和埃及美女哀荷（Io）相戀的故事，較相似，和雅歌所說的大異其趣。所以雅歌不可能是祀神曲。

B　是寓言詩嗎？

把雅歌看做寓言詩，是很早的事了。猶太教和基督教都非常喜歡把雅歌寓言化。在 Talmud（公元一五零年至五百年間的一部律法書，意譯作 to learn）裏便發現有這樣的解釋，至於 T rgum（自從尼希米時代起，猶太人要認識聖經，都要靠專家宣讀並解釋，因他們已忘記自己的民族語言了。這類的解釋後來編纂成爲典籍）裏面，指新郎是耶和華，新婦是猶太民族。雅歌全書是寓言方式描繪出猶太民族自從出埃及，彌賽亞來臨，直到第三聖殿（Third Temple 也叫做 Herod's Temple，建於公元前二十年，完成於公元六十四年，毀於公元七十年）

時代，這段時間和上帝的關係的經歷。

另一種寓言性的解釋是富神祕性的。主要人物是所羅門（Lmnanuel leen Solomon）他說：雅歌是一部富有人生智慧的書。

今日猶太學人雖不再見有這樣的風氣，但這樣的解釋，却成爲正統派的解釋。

到了基督教的神學家手中，就更加光怪陸離了。雅歌最初被認爲所羅門和埃及公主締結良緣的婚歌，基此，遂造成較深的寓言意味。那新郎被解釋作基督，新婦被解釋作教會，及每一信徒。解釋新婦作教會的有洋羅姆（Jerome）奧古斯汀，（Augustine），提奧勞累特（Theodoret），約翰‧衛斯理（John Wesley），和爲 King James 英譯本寫每章提要的作者。解釋新婦作信徒個人的有：格黎哥利（Gregory of Nyssa）默那地（Bernard of Clairnant）和斯圖亞特（Moses Stuart）等。

羅馬天主教則把新婦解釋爲童貞女馬利亞。

根據勿萊德曼(Thomas Brightman)的舉例，一：1至四：6，是在敍說律法時代的會幕與聖殿，從大衞至穌耶的受死；四：7至八：14敍述傳福音的教會，從主後廿四年至基督再來。依照路得馬丁（Martin Luther）的說法：新婦象徵國家，全本集子是所羅門向上帝歌頌的樂章，上帝使他的臣民效忠於他（本段取材自 The Interpreter's Bible Volume, 5:92, 93）。

關於寓言詩，聖經中的先知文學可以說是最豐富的淵藪。

29

兹舉何西亞二：2至4節為例，英文標準新譯本作：

> P ead with your mother, plead—
>> for she is not my wife,
>> and I am not her husband—
>> that she put away her harlotry from
>> her face,
>> and her adultery from between her
>> breasts;
> Lest I strip her naked,
>> and make her as in the day she was born,
>> and make her like a wilderness,
>> and set her like a parched land,
>> and slay her with thirst.
> Upon her children also I will have no pity.
>> because they are children of harlotry.

兹以騷體翻譯如下：

> 與爾母抗辯兮
> 蓋彼非余之妻
> 余豈彼之夫兮
> 彼淫蕩而沈迷
> 幸除其面上之尤態兮
> 去彼胸脯之妖姿
> 恐余剝脫其衣裳兮
> 使赤體如初生之時

30

令乾渴以自斃兮·

如荒漠旱地之可悲

余不恤其所產兮

從邪慾而生諸小兒

又以西結卅七章以平原上枯骨的復甦而喻以色列的復興，都是有名的寓言詩。

中國的寓言詩也非常發達，如論語微子的接輿歌：

鳳兮，鳳兮

何德之衰

往者不可諫

來者猶可追

己而，己而

今之從政者殆而

這首詩，充滿了道家憤世疾俗的思想，譏笑儒家，以鳳兮喻聖人。

又如孺子歌：

滄浪之水清兮

可以濯我纓

滄浪之水濁兮

可以濯我足

——孟子離婁

詩經中比，興的詩更多是寓言式的。楚辭尤其是著名於善用寓言，如九章的涉江：

余幼好此奇服兮

年既老而不衰

帶長鋏之陸離兮

冠切雲之崔嵬

被明月兮佩寶璐

世溷濁而莫余知兮

吾方高馳而不顧

駕青虬兮驂白螭

吾與重華遊兮瑤之圃

登崑崙兮食玉英

與天地兮比壽

與日月兮齊光

·················

亂曰：

鸞鳥鳳凰

日以遠兮

燕雀烏鵲

巢堂壇兮

露申辛夷

死林薄兮

腥臊並御

芳不得薄兮

陰陽易位

時不當兮

懷信侘傺

32

忽乎吾將行兮

幾乎全用寓言的方式出之。

雅歌和何西亞或以西結等先知的寓言詩性質不同，和接輿歌，涉江等也不類，和滄浪歌就有點近似。

滄浪歌在楚辭的漁父辭中也用到。那漁父唱這首歌的寓意很顯然：滄浪之水清的時候，可以洗我的帽纓，是說太平的日子，天下有道，我們可以出來任事；滄浪之水濁的時候，可以洗我們的脚，就是說，天下無道，我們可以潔身以去，不與世事。

但在孔子的立場看，我們立身處世，要像滄浪水清之時，可以使人洗濯帽纓，不要像滄浪水濁之時，讓人家在那裏洗足。

做這首童謠的，原沒有什麼寓意，但聽這曲的是孔子，用「小子聽之，清斯濯纓，濁斯濯足矣，自取之也」一言加上去，就變成寓言詩了。

雅歌也是這樣的，本來是男女純潔的戀歌，經過後人用以比喩宗教上的奧義，便變成寓言詩了。

請看詩經鄭風中的「風雨」：

風雨凄凄　　雞鳴喈喈
旣見君子　　云胡不夷

風雨瀟瀟　　雞鳴膠膠
旣見君子　　云胡不瘳

<pre>
        風雨如晦   雞鳴不已
        旣見君子   云胡不喜
</pre>

這十足是一首戀歌，描寫一位女子在風雨交加，白晝如黑夜的時候，突然遇見她心所愛的，大喜過望的心情。但後人把這詩寓言化了，阮籍說：「君子在何許，曠世未合並」！陶潛的「靄靄停雲」：

<pre>
        靄靄停雲   茫茫時雨
        八表同昏   平陸伊阻
        靜寄東軒   春醪獨撫
        良朋悠邈   搔袖延佇
</pre>

就是竊取斯意。

　　顧炎武說：明淸之際就是「風雨如晦，雞鳴不已」的時代。「風雨」這詩本沒有此意，後人把它寓言化了。雅歌亦然。

C　是戲劇嗎？

　　解釋雅歌是劇本的始於希臘文譯經時代，在希臘文譯本圈內找到這說法的來歷。最初主是說的是兩部希臘文譯本：Codex Cinaiticus 和 Codex Alexandrinus，是四世紀和五世紀的產物，裏面附加了許多眉批。

　　Ethiopic 譯本是根據希臘文譯本的，更進一步把雅歌分爲五段，成爲五個劇本。當然了，不必等到路得馬丁的改革教會，雅歌是劇本的理論就有了很完全的發展。裏面有兩個主角說：男的是所羅門，有時飾作牧羊人，女的是書念女郎亞比煞。雅歌就是這兩人互相愛慕的戀歌。許多學者曾懸揣這劇本

的佈景和扮演的方法，最普遍的是黎里茲（Franz Delitzsch, 1875），他把雅歌分爲六幕劇，每幕各有兩場。

　　兩主角的解釋自始就非常有力，但它改作爲戲劇，在術語上是矛盾的。這歌集如果是戲劇，何以內容上沒有戲劇性的發展？裏面也不只是兩個人的事。如果只有兩個主角，它就缺乏倫理上的目的。

　　爲補足這樣理論的不足，又產生了三角戀的戲劇說。

　　伊斯拉（Ibn Izra）顯然是第一個創三角戀戲劇說的人，主角是王和兩個情人（鄉村女郎和牧羊人）。這說沒有到耶可比（J. F. Ecobi, 1771）時代便非常廣被了。後來有個作者把新生命注入戲劇說中，這人就是依瓦奧特（Hinrich Ewald, 1826），他把雅歌分爲五幕劇，每幕一場或一場以上。劇情是說所羅門王逗引一美麗的書念女郎，想要贏得她的芳心和愛情，她却始終不變地愛她那個牧羊的情郎。那麼，這詩歌所說的便不是夫婦之愛，像兩主角說所持的，而是一種純眞的愛了。這樣的理論把所羅門安放在不光榮的地位上，不會是正確的，因爲猶太的拉比定不肯把這樣的書編入聖經中。瓦特曼（Leroy Waterman)引一個猶太經典的編者的說法：這集子是一個北方的作者侮蔑所羅門王的作品。但何以猶太人要收這不甚重要的經書在聖經裏呢？戲劇在猶太正統派眼中是不合適的，益使這理論無法建立。如果作者有意寫詩劇，他要用方言，而不用雅言，對於扮演者的身份，台詞的配置，時間的連續，地場和情節的交換，都要非常的顯豁，而不是那麼隱晦了（取材自 The Interpreter's Bible Volume 5, p. 93）。

聞一多氏「九歌古歌舞劇懸解」一文，把九歌這十首歌舞劇本，用近代的文學手腕加以調整（ arrangement ）。茲錄湘君如下，讀者在這裏就很難看出它和雅歌有什麼不同：

　　人物：湘君　　湘公子　　車夫　　男侍數人　　女子甲
　　　　　女子乙　　船娘　　女侍數人

　　江心一個小島，島上蘭莖叢中藏着一座小得幾乎像玩具樣的廟子。

　　是一個深秋的黃昏，落葉在西風中旋舞。

　　樹葉不時閃着「神光」。剛從島後石灘間迂迴地來到島上的車子，走到廟前停下了。車上的人，除了湘君，都上廟前來。湘君佇立在車上，吹着鳳簫，簫停了，遠處一個女高音開始唱道：

　　君不行兮夷猶，蹇誰留兮中洲！

（一隻船滿載着婦女，從右側出現，向着島這邊划來了。）

　女甲：

　　美要眇兮宜修，沛吾乘兮桂舟。

　　令沅湘兮無波，使江水兮安流，

　　望夫君兮未來，吹參差兮誰思！

　　（湘君看見船來了，急忙跳下車來，跑到水邊）

　湘君：

　　駕飛龍兮北征，邅吾道兮洞庭，

　　薜荔柏兮蕙綢，蓀橈兮蘭旌。

　　望涔陽兮極浦，橫大江兮揚靈，（閃着神光。）

　　揚靈兮未極，女嬋媛兮爲余太息。

36

（船慢慢靠近岸旁停下了）。

女甲：

（掩面悲泣）横流涕兮潺湲，隱思君兮陫側。

湘君：

桂櫂兮蘭枻，斲冰兮積雪。

桂櫂兮蘭枻，斲冰兮積雪！

采薜荔兮水中，搴芙蓉兮木末（有些氣憤）。

心不同兮媒勞，恩不甚兮輕絕！

女甲：

石瀨兮淺淺，飛龍兮翩翩。

石瀨兮淺淺，飛龍兮翩翩。

交不忠兮怨長，期不信兮告余以不閒！

（湘君以謝罪的姿式，走上前，把女子甲扶下船來。

二人攜手向花草叢中走去了。）

湘君：

朝騁騖兮江皋，夕弭節兮北渚。

鳥次兮屋上，水周兮堂下。

捐余袂兮江中，遺余佩兮醴浦，

采芳洲兮杜若，將以遺兮下女，

時不可兮再得，聊逍遙兮容與。

湘君，女甲：

鳥次兮屋上，水周兮堂下，

時不可兮再得，聊逍遙兮容與！

（燈光熄，幕下；隨即升起，燈光又明。）

甲三一二——三一五。

如果把雅歌加以調整（arrangement），也不難得到這樣的形式。但所不同的是九歌本質上是楚國人淫祀（漢書地理志說：「楚人信巫鬼而重淫祀」）的歌劇，而雅歌是純粹的戀歌。國語楚語：

「古者神民不雜，民之精爽不攜貳者，而又能齊肅中正。……如是，神明降之，在男曰覡，在女曰巫。」

說文：

巫，祝也；女能事無形以舞降神者也。象兩人褒舞形。

覡，能齊肅事神明者。

商書伊尹訓：「恆舞于宮，酣歌于室，時謂之「巫風」。陳太姬好巫，而民淫祀，詩稱「擊鼓於宛邱之上，婆娑於枌樹之下。」

這樣，聞一多把九歌改裝（arrangement）爲現代的歌舞劇是有根據的。雅歌除第六章第十五節提到跳舞以外，再也沒有看到跳舞的事。雅歌非祀神曲，前段已詳論之。兩主角，三主角戀愛的戲劇說沒有根據，又難自圓其說：所以裏面雖有許多戲劇性的對白，却只能認爲具有詩經十五國風那山歌和褒歌的本色，和九歌情節離奇，神祕浪漫的歌劇形式不同科。

D 雅歌與智慧

雅歌在聖經中是列入第三部門，一邊貼近詩篇，耶利米哀歌；另一邊又與箴言，傳道書，約伯記等同科。這一門在聖經裏是很重要的部分，是智慧的淵府（repository of hokmah or wisdom）。智慧不僅是文學的一支，而且包括文化上一切的技能

與藝術。舉凡建築，冶金，航海，縫製，魔術及治國的才能，均可解釋作 hakamim "wise" 據希伯來拉比的說法 hakamah 也用作「助產婆」。

　　希伯來古代生活資料被摧毀之後，hokmah 原來的意義也就被忘却而泯滅，它較具有神學的意味指出形而上與倫理上的眞理，穿上文學的外衣，都是後來發展的結果。它在字義學上的生長，由具體漸趨於抽象。確認希臘文中的 sophia，其含義也是一樣地繁複。這情形在語言上是非常普遍的。sophia 使用於 Hephaestus，是火和藝術之神，使用於 Athena 和 Daedalus，是工匠和藝術家，使用於 Telchines 這原始民族中，有三種意思：一，耕種土地者和諸神之服役者。二，術士，嫉妬之鬼，他有權力呼喚雨雪和雹，以毀壞動物和植物。三，從事於鍊冶銅和鐵的技工。普通 sophia 被用於類似木工，駕車，醫藥和手術的技巧，又使用於卓越的歌唱，音樂和詩篇。這希臘字的本義是手工與藝術上的技巧和聰明（ cleverness and skill in handicraft and art ），引伸爲日常生活上的技能，正確的判斷，政治上的智慧與設施。(skill in matters of common life, sound judgment, practical and political wisdom)，終成爲學問，智慧，和哲學（ learning, wisdom and philosophy ）。形容詞的 Sophos 產生同樣的意義，使用於雕刻工人，築籬和掘溝的人，但最主要是形容詩人，音樂家。名詞 Sophistes 是指雕刻或藝術的專家，由現存的典籍看出它是應用於占卜者，烹調者，政治家，而也使用於詩人和音樂家。從柏拉圖以還，通用的意義是職業的藝術的教師。

Hokmah 最常被用於代表詩與歌的藝術，包括用口唱出，用樂器彈出，或編製詩歌與樂章，這些且常由一個人包辦，需要極高度的技能。耶利米九章十七節記載那些在喪禮中善唱哀歌的婦女叫做 Hakamoth。

歌和智慧是這麼相近，甚至兩個名詞可以互換。王上四：29—34記着：「上帝賜給所羅門極大的智慧聰明……他的智慧……勝過以斯拉人以探，並瑪曷的兒子希幔，……他作箴言三千句，詩歌一千零五首……天下列王聽見所羅門的智慧，就都差人來聽他的智慧話。」

以探、希幔被描繪爲聰明智慧者的代表，而他們是第一聖殿時代的音樂大宗師，唱歌的能手。歷代志上十五章十九節：「派歌唱的希幔，亞薩，以探，敲鑼鈸大發響聲，」是其明證。再者：上面的記載把箴言和詩歌對舉，可見二者關係的密切了。

先知巴蘭之歌叫 Māshāl 其原義爲比喻，或者那詩中充滿了比喻（民數記廿三章廿四節）。但其本質上該是歌的同義語（is a synonym for song）。民數記廿一：27至30那首戰爭的史詩叫 Moshelim，Hidāh 這詞（猜謎，神祕的說法），和 Māshāl 在一起，是配弦琴的歌（詩篇四九篇四節）。新近由 Ugaritic 的資料證實聖經的傳統，除掉年代的錯誤，指明這種歌唱的組織極其古老。事實上他們產生在迦南人的時代。

智慧的文學開始是具有世俗化的調子，漸漸着上宗教的色彩。從埃及東方的智慧（Oriental wisdom）的年表清楚地看

40

出來，它的宗教色彩是後來才顯現的。以色列人也是如此，腓法（Pfeiffer）正確地說「我們確信那（智慧的）世俗化是發達於敬神之前」。最早的希伯來箴言或智慧的片斷，被錄在史乘上的，全是世俗化的。

和智慧文學同樣地發展，或可假定是智慧的旁支，叫做Shir，它包括詩歌與音樂。歌使用於宗教儀式中，成爲重要的部分，但決不限獻祭，節期等宗教活動範圍。事實上是和生活一樣地擴張，好比戰爭與勝利，開一口井，收穫葡萄及穀物，宴飲娛賓，死亡的哀榮與悲悼等。

無疑地，許多詩歌具有民族的意義，戰爭勝利，而著上宗教色彩，如「海之歌」（出十五），「底波拉之歌」（士五）。但民廿一：十七，撒下一：十八，等都是純粹世俗化的詩歌。

雅歌就是具備純粹世俗化的詩歌，裏面充滿愛情和獻媚，它更能引起人類的詩意和音樂感。在這範圍內，性慾和肉體成爲很重要的部分，傳統的宗教因素是極難立足其間的。埃及古代戀歌和亞圭丹（Akkadian）的文學留到今天的，和當代亞刺伯農民與市民生活一樣，加強這個論點，且成爲了解聖經中詩歌之鑰。

（本段取材於Gordis: The Song of Songs, PP. 13—16）

四　類型

A　雅歌是情歌彙編

如果不存成見的話，用純粹客觀的態度去審察，不難看出雅歌是一集情歌的彙編。十五世紀的 Middle High German 譯

41

本就透露這樣的看法；它把雅歌分爲五十四首詩。許多現代的學者一脈相承地接受這論旨，只是區分的方法不同。

一八九三年惠茲底因（J．G．Wetzstein）（波斯駐大馬士磕的領事），曾往前大邁進了一步，叫我們要注意敍利亞農民婚禮的習俗，在婚筵上那一對璧人要坐於「寶座」上，卽所謂「王」和「后」了；同時客人唱歌褒美新婦和新郎。在某種情形之下新娘實行「劍舞」。雅歌有許多段落被學者認爲是這類的婚歌。

在結婚時褒美新娘是第二聖殿時代猶太人的習俗，這種技藝是屬乎 Hokmah 的，一部分是 Talmudic（猶太宗教法典）的傳統習俗。同樣的方法實行於歐洲，由詼諧的丑角或唱歌者扮演於婚禮中，直到今天。

另一方面，許多抒情詩在雅歌裏和婚禮或夫婦之愛渺不相涉，正確的結論乃雅歌和詩篇一樣是集子，充滿了情感的音調，包括愛情的渴慕和滿足，撒嬌與戀念，分離與重圓，求愛和成親。

分首的標準是基於主題、觀點，背景的轉移，形式的變易。但這軌範很難完全靠得住而受人家所公認；許多要靠文學的經驗和識力，如依賴智識，或註釋之類。註釋是把原文的眞實性重行陳述的一種藝術，是建基在科學智識上的。

B 分章擧隅

雅歌第一章九至十七節常被註釋家認爲是一首詩。可是在第九節裏講到法老車前的駿馬，好像是以南部巴勒斯坦爲背景。在十四節中又提到隱基底的葡萄園，這地方是死海的西

岸，明明是猶大的南部。而底下十七節敍述愛人們幽會於樹林中，「以香柏爲房屋的棟樑」，可是巴勒斯坦的南部沒有出產香柏木。所以這幾節應該分爲兩首詩：第九至十四；十五至十七。

前一首是敍述那靜女佩戴着豪華的首飾（九至十一節），那個吉士稱爲「王」（十二節），當然是新郎。他或者是在婚期中的宴會向他的新娘說話：「你的兩顋……你的頸項……我們要……」，因爲她是在他的朋友們面前表演的，所以用多數的「我們」。十二節和十三節分明在襯托出性愛：「一囊沒藥正像心愛的，在我胸脯間棲息」。下一首詩却很簡單地描繪着愛人們在戶外幽會的情形，就不是新郎和新婦的事了。

C 雅歌的分類與題旨

甲 渴慕的詩歌

愛的宣召（一：二至四節）

田舍女郎（一：五至六節）

情郎在那裏（一：七至八節）

大膽的宣佈（二：四至七節）

若你做我的兄弟（八：一至四節）

讓我聽到你的聲音（八：十三至十四節）

乙，實現的詩歌

愛情的欄柵（對白）（四：十二至五：一節）

多廢可喜的愛情（七：七至十節）

靜女的諾言（七：十一至十四節）

蘋菓樹下之戀（對白）（八：五節）

43

投降（二：十六至十七節）

　　丙　褒美靜女的詩歌

動人的裝飾（一：九至十四節）

全美的愛人（四：一至七節）

令人消魂的愛情（四：九至十一節）

美的魔力（六：四至七節）

獨一無二（六：八至九節）

　　丁　互相褒美的對話詩歌

香柏作牆垣（一：十五至十七節）

愛人的比喻（二：一至三節）

愛人的歡迎（二：十四至十五節）

　　戊　大自然懷抱中的戀情

歌唱的季節已來臨（二：八至十三節）

山岳的呼喚（四：八節）

愛情的曙光（六：十至十二節）

　　己　美夢的詩歌

失愛者之夢（三：一至五節）

愛情的苦樂（五：二節至六：三節）

　　庚　愛情的偉大

愛的烙印（八：六至七節）

最美的葡萄園（八：十一至十二節）

　　辛　求愛與成親的詩歌

所羅門結婚進行曲（三：六至十一節）

女郎的舞姿（七：一至六節）

44

愛情的堅壘（八：八至十節）

壬　愛情的滋味

愛情的苦樂（五：二節至六：三節）

附註：「愛情的苦樂」一首是集中最長的詩歌，是作者刻意經營而成者；可分爲三部分：A，夢境（五：二），賣俏撒嬌（五：三）渴慕（五：四）；B，褒美良人的歌詞（五：十至十六節）；C，愛情的禮讚（六：二至三節）。

D　幾個特徵

1・「我指着羚羊，或田野的母鹿，囑咐你們」（二：7；三：5），此中的羚羊和母鹿是象徵性的寫法，隱喩着靈雅而可愛的女人。伊迷寧（Ebeling）氏提醒我們注意到巴比倫的魔術儀式中，綁一隻羚羊在床頭，一隻公山羊在脚上。目的是：「我的丈夫會像公山羊這樣地愛我」。但這和一神論的希伯來人的習性不類。

希臘人常指動植物發誓：「指着狗」，「指着鵝」，「指着樹」。希臘哲學家禁止這樣的作風，顯示他們不曾故意指動物而發誓，像指神祇一般，但用動物作神祇的代用品。這不單是辯解而已，且反映他們對一種不會實現的誓言的影響力存着畏懼的心理。

在拉比的誓詞彙編中，曾用「馬」（gee）代「耶穌」（Jesus），「聖牛」(hloy cow)代「聖基督」（Holy Christ）；常避諱不敢提上帝的聖名。希伯來人認爲最嚴重的名字就是上帝，如"⸺y the Lord of Hosts'或"by the Almighty"（萬軍之耶利華，或全能者）。關於這點，是出埃及記廿章七節明文

45

規定要敬畏這聖名，不得隨便稱呼；以斯帖記和傳道書已反映出這傾向，編纂詩篇，及拉比文學中也很明顯地有如此的忌諱。肉慾方面的愛，自然更加不敢觸犯上帝的聖名，要避免指他起誓了。

2‧埃及人和米索不達米亞人很喜歡打獵。埃及的黃金時代（the Golden Age）曾有這樣的抒情詩：

> 那是多麼好
>
> 若你跟着我
>
> 當我張了羅

張羅是要捕雀的，而他的意思是要設圈套叫愛人投入他的掌握中。聖經裏有寧錄，以掃是打獵的能手，而以色列民族却沒有打獵的生活，所以雅歌沒有這資料。

3‧擬人的文學手法在埃及很是普遍，如「園中之樹」（The tree in the garden）有「樹說」（The tree speaketh）的寫法，雅歌也沒有。

4‧喝酒的生活在以色列是很普遍的。雅歌中常提到酒。

5‧學者曾提以「妹子」喻所愛的女郎，是受埃及的影響。其實這是枝節而牽強的說法。

6‧杜爾辛萊（Tur-Sinai）叫我們要注意八：9：

> 如果他是一座城，
>
> 我要造銀梁麗去衝撞；
>
> 如果他是一重門，
>
> 我們要拿香柏盾去圍攻。

亞述人防兒童哭鬧的咒語中有：

如他是一隻狗，

擲一口吃的給牠！

如他是一隻鳥，

用土塊拋牠！

如他是一個淘氣的孩子，

要用 Anu 和 Antu 的誓語對付他！

這兩種的句法相似，但不能說雅歌是抄襲亞述人咒語的腔調。

比方五：9--16節：

你所愛的有甚麼過人的地方，

啊！你這最美麗的女郎？

....

我的愛人英俊又殷紅

萬人比不上他的高風。

我的五古譯文是：

若比他吉士	所愛究何殊……
所愛勝萬人	面白雙頰朱……
其首若精金	髮鬚密氈氄
色澤玄以黑	玄黑似慈烏
眼如溪邊鴿	開對靈源立
配置真適宜	沐浴以乳汁
醸猶香花畦	其氣郁且烈
唇乃百合花	沒藥液外泄
手臂黃金管	嵌玉白勝雪
象牙雕作身	鑲石藍而潔

47

脛寄精金座	宛然石膏柱
貌肖利巴嫩	秀於香柏樹
口吻甜且美	全然可愛慕
邱城諸女子	敢煩爲關注
斯乃儂良人	相知已有素

和樂府清商曲中大曲的「陌上桑」那好女秦羅敷襃美其夫
婿，如出一轍：

……何用識夫婿	白馬從驪駒……
青絲繫馬尾	黃金絡馬頭
腰間鹿盧劍	可值千萬餘
十五府小吏	二十朝大夫
三十侍中郎	四十專城居
爲人潔白皙	鬑鬑頗有鬚
盈盈公府步	冉冉府中趨
坐中千餘人	皆言夫婿殊

到底是誰效法誰呢？人類的智慧發展到某一階段會產生這樣的
襃歌，東方西方都是一樣的，殊不必硬說這一定是誰抄襲誰的。

7·雅歌是一部強調人類至性之愛的歌集。這是人性向另
一極端去發展的高度表現。猶太民族崇奉上帝，一切以神旨爲
依皈，顯出他們有向心力，有歸宿，但又不能抹殺人性。人性
傾向肉慾，傾向屬物質的美感與快感。歌底斯說：雅歌找不到
貞節與倫理，只有嫉妒與無信。話是有根據的，如八：6至7
節：

置余爾心頭	銘鏤作印誌

或在腕臂間　　鐫刻成戳記
愛情強固死亡境
媄恨凶殘陰府地
厭餕是雷鞭　　無上熱且熾
衆水淹之不熄滅
洪流沖之益縱恣
傾家以求之　　必爲所厭棄

　　但對上帝之愛和對肉慾之愛，在象徵性和寓言性的解釋中得到統一，因爲這兩種愛都是人類至性之愛的表現，一個健全的人都得具備這兩面，缺一不可。拿雅歌以況喩神和人和教會之愛，雖然不是原來的要素，至少和顧炎武解釋「風雨」一詩的意味同樣深厚，令人盪氣迴腸呢！

　　附註：第四各節的資料都是譯自歌底斯 ："The Song of Songs" 導言的。但我的見解和他有許多出入的地方。

　　於慶得男嬰之次日完稿 ，時爲主曆一九五九年七月 二十日。

廣場與鬧市　尋求情所鍾
康衢足跡遍　無處覓郎蹤

一凌黑門頂　窺探獅子窩

遠征豹子巚　萬劫眼底過

譯譯
英漢
斯體
底話
戲白

THE SONG OF SONGS, WHICH IS SOLOMON'S

CHAPTER ONE

THE CALL TO LOVE

In passionate accents, the beloved voices her desire for the presence of her bridegroom, who is here called "king," in accordance with a common West-Semitic and Jewish usage.

This song emantes not from the countryside, but from the city. Hence the background of many-chambered houses, the abundance of wine and oil and the presence of many maidens (1:2-4).

Let me drink of the kisses of his mouth,

For thy love is better than wine!

Thine oils are a delight to inhale,

Thy presence—as oil wafted about,

Therefore do the maidens love thee.

Draw me after thee, let us hasten—

The king has brought me to his chambers,

Saying, "We will rejoice and be merry with thee!"

We shall inhale thy love rather than wine!

As fine wine do they love thee.

所羅門之歌　　歌中之雅歌

一　愛的宣召

惹人愛的人兒用熱情的音調說出她渴慕情郎的出現，在這裏他被稱爲「王」，是沿襲閃族西支和猶太人的用法。

這詩歌不是田園詩，而是從都市裏溢出來的。基於它的背景有許多內室的房宅，豐盛的美酒與膏油，並有無算的童女（1：2—4）。

> 讓我酣歔他嘴上的甜吻，
>
> 因您的愛情勝過春醪，
>
> 您的膏油聞了令人魂消，
>
> 您出現——像香氣浮飄，
>
> 自然衆童女都愛上您了。

> 吸引我跟着您，快些——
>
> 王領我進他的椒房，
>
> 說，「我們要與你共歡暢！」
>
> 我們寧喝您的愛情過於瓊漿
>
> 她們愛您像酒醴甜又香。

CHAPTER TWO

THE RUSTIC MAIDEN

*A country girl addresses the sophisticated women of the capital
with a mixture of naivete and coquetry, of modesty and pride. Her
skin, unlike that of the well-kept women of the capital, is dark.
She has been exposed to the sun's rays, because she has been com-
pelled to guard the vineyards of her brothers, who were angry with
her. Their displeasure stemmed from the fact that she had left
her own "vineyard" unguarded, being too prodigal with her favors
(1:5-6).*

Swarthy am I, but comely, O daughters of Jerusalem,

Swarthy as Kedar's tents,

Comely as Solomonic hangings.

Do not look askance upon me, for being swarthy,

For the sun has tanned me;

My brothers were incensed against me,

They set me a keeper over the vineyards;

But my own vineyard I did not keep.

二　田舍女郎

　　一個村女用質樸而傲岸，並天眞的嬌態向矯飾的首都女人們陳辭。她的肌膚，不像城市婦女的受庇蔭，是黝黑的。她常暴露在陽光之下，因爲兄弟們逼她去看守他們的葡萄園，且向她發慈；而她自己的葡萄園卻沒有看守，太浪費了她的心血（1：5—6）。

　　　　郇城的女子們，我黝黑而秀茂，

　　　　黝黑得像基達的帳幕，

　　　　秀麗得像所羅門的羅幕

　　　　別睨視我，以我黝黑，

　　　　是太陽曬我成墨色；

　　　　兄弟們向我怒赫赫，

　　　　強我負看守葡萄園之責；

　　　　我自己的卻看守不得。

55

CHAPTER THREE

TELL ME WHERE MY LOVE

The maiden pleads with her lover, to tell her where he is guarding his flocks. She gives him a gentle warning that if she must seek him herself, his fellow—shepherds are likely to make overtures for her affection (1:7-8).

Tell me, O thou whom I love,

Where dost thou pasture thy sheep,

Where dost thou let them lie at noon?

Why, indeed, should I be a wanderer

Among the flocks of thy comrades,

Who would say to me:

"If thou knowest not, fairest among women,

Follow the footprints of the sheep,

And pasture thy kids

Near the tents of the shepherds."

三　情郎在那裏

　　這位女郎向她的愛人請求，要說明在那裏牧放他的羊羣。她給他一個溫柔的聲告，如她自己去尋找他，他的牧羊伙伴會爲她的熱情而給予提示（1：7--8）。

> 　　告訴我，我所鍾愛的；
>
> 　　您的羊羣在那兒牧放，
>
> 　　亭午叫羊歇何方？
>
> 　　怎麼，眞是，叫我像個人彷徨
>
> 　　在您夥伴羣羊裏擯，
>
> 　　他們要告訴我：
>
> 　　「女人中之最美麗的，若你不懂，別慌，
>
> 　　只跟着羊羣的腳蹤，
>
> 　　牧放你的小山羊，
>
> 　　在牧人帳棚之旁。」

CHAPTER FOUR

BEDECKED IN CHARM

In this duet, the locale of which is southern Palestine, the "king" praises the beauty of his bride, bedecked in gold and silver ornaments, and compares her to a steed in Pharaoh's chariots. The comparison, somewhat strange to our habits of thought, is characteristically Semitic. It should be recalled that the horse was not a beast of burden in the Orient, but the cherished companion of kings and nobles in war and the chase. The bride responds by extolling the joys of love with her "king" (1:9-14).

THE BRIDEGROOM:
To a steed in Pharaoh's chariots
Do I compare thee, my beloved.
Thy neck, with strings of jewels.
Thy neck, with strings of jewels.
Golden beads shall we make thee
With studs of silver.

THE BRIDE:
While the king was on his couch,
My nard gave forth its fragrance.
A bag of myrrh is my beloved,
Lying between by breasts.
A cluster of henna is my beloved to me
From the vineyards of En-gedi.

四　動人的裝飾

　　這對話的地點是巴勒斯坦南部，「王」讚稱其新娘的美貌，有金銀的首飾，儗她作法老車上的駿馬。這樣的比喻，在我們的風俗中感到陌生，卻是閃族的典型。要明白東方人不把馬當做服苦的牲畜，而是王者貴族們戰爭追奔逐北的良伴。新娘歌頌愛情的喜樂以囘答她的「王」（1：9—14）。

　　　　新郎：像法老車上的一匹駿馬——

　　　　　　　心愛的，我這樣地儗你。

　　　　　　　你的兩頰因耳飾而華麗，

　　　　　　　你頸上繞着串串的寶玉。

　　　　　　　我們要給你加上金珠

　　　　　　　釘上了銀飾。

　　　　新娘：當王在他的榻上，

　　　　　　　我的哪噠發出香氣。

　　　　　　　一囊沒藥正像心愛的，

　　　　　　　在我胸脯間棲息。

　　　　　　　我看心上人是一叢鳳仙花

　　　　　　　在隱基底葡萄園裏。

59

CHAPTER FIVE

OUR WALLS ARE CEDARS

This simple lyric is of North—Israelite origin. The lovers make their tryst in the forest, with the cedars and cypresses as their home (1:15-17).

THE LOVER:	Thou art fair, my beloved, thou art fair,
	Thine eyes are doves.
THE BELOVED:	Thou art handsome, my beloved, yea sweet,
	And our couch is green.
BOTH:	The beams of our house are cedars,
	And our rafters are cypresses.

五　香柏作垣墻

這簡單的抒情詩是以色列北部的本色。愛人們幽會於叢林裏，用香柏樹和絲杉當他們的家（1：15—17）。

男唱：你瑰麗，心愛的，你瑰麗，
　　　你的眼睛像鴿子。
女唱：您英俊，心愛的，眞甜蜜，
　　　芳茵做我們的牀榻。
合唱：我們的屋棟是香柏，
　　　絲杉做我們的椽桷。

CHAPTER SIX

WHO IS LIKE MY LOVE

In this brief duet, the maiden describes her charms in modest terms which the lover turns into a triumphant praise of her beauty. She counters by extolling his handsome presence, describing the joy she finds in his company (2:1-3).

THE MAIDEN: I am but a rose in Sharon,

A lily of the valleys.

THE YOUTH: As a lily among thorns,

So is my beloved among the young women.

THE MAIDEN: As an apple-tree among the trees of the wood,

So is my love among the young men.

Under its shadow I delight to sit,

And its fruit is sweet to my taste.

六　愛人的比喻

　　這段對話裏，那女郎用謙遜的詞語述說自己的可愛，她的愛人卻把它們變成誇飾她美姿的詞歌。她也讚稱他的俊邁，承認在其友伴中找到了喜樂（2：1—3）。

　　　女郎：我乃沙崙一朵玫瑰，

　　　　　　一朵百合處幽谷。

　　　少年：所愛的在少女中，

　　　　　　像朵荊棘中的百合。

　　　女郎：愛人於少年中，

　　　　　　像棵蘋果立於林薄。

　　　　　　心花怒放地坐在它蔭下，

　　　　　　它的果實嘗起來甜如蜜！

CHAPTEER SEVEN

LOVE'S PROUD PROCLAMATION

The maiden proudly announces her love before all who are assembled in the tavern, and asks for refreshment, for she is faint through passion. She adjures the daughters of Jerusalem by a solemn oath to leave the lovers undisturbed, till their desire be spent (2:4-7).

He has brought me to the banquet-hall,

With his banner of love above me.

Strengthen me with dainties, sustain me with apples;

For I am love-sick.

His left hand is beneath my head,

While his right embraces me.

I adjure you, O daughters of Jerusalem,

By the gazelles and the hinds of the field,

That you disturb not, nor interrupt our love,

Until it be satiated.

七　大膽的宣佈

女郎在酒店的羣衆面前自得地宣佈她嘗到的愛，呼籲使她精力恢復，她因性愛而頭昏眼花。她用嚴肅的誓言懇求耶路撒冷衆女子勿打擾愛人們，讓他們的渴念饜足（2：4—7）。

> 他領我進宴會場，
>
> 他的愛旗在我頂上飄揚。
>
> 用蘋果支撐我，用庶羞叫我康強；
>
> 因爲愛情叫我盪氣迴腸。
>
> 他的左手放在我頭下，
>
> 他的右手把我摟住。
>
> 我向你們呼籲，「耶城的衆女子，
>
> 指着田野間的羚羊與母鹿，
>
> 你們別攪擾，別打斷我們的愛，
>
> 等到它滿足。」

CHAPTER EIGHT
THE TIME OF SINGING IS COME

This lyric is perhaps the most beautiful expression of love in the spring to be found in literature. It is worth noting that the point of origin is the city rather than the counttry. That nature discloses her charms primarily to the urban dweller rather than to the rustic has long been suspected. The appreciation of nature and the creation of nature-poetry are the products of urban culture, whether it be ancient Israel, the Hellenistic Age, the Silver Age of Roman literature, or the modern Romantic movement.

The city maiden, ensconced in her house, sees her lover coming to her and calling her to go out with him to the country-side, so that they may greet the spring in all its loveliness (2:8-13).

Hark! my beloved! here he comes,
Leaping over the mountains, skipping over the hills.
My beloved is like a gazelle or a young hart;
Behold, he stands behind our wall,
Looking through the windows,
Peering through the lattices.
My beloved spoke, saying unto me:
"Rise up, my love, my fair one, and come away.
For lo, the winter is past,
The rain is over and gone;
The flowers have appeared on the earth;
The time of singing is come,
And the voice of the turtle-dove is heard in our land.
The fig-tree puts forth her green fruits,
And the vines in blossom give forth their fragrance.
Arise, my love, my fair one· and come away."

八　歌唱的季節已來臨

　　這首也許可說是文學上表達春天的戀情最美麗的抒情詩了。值得注意的是它的發祥地是城市而不是鄉村。大自然將它的美景昭示給都市的居民，而不顯給質樸的鄉下佬，這觀點早就有人懷疑了。但鑑賞自然和田園詩的創作，是都市的產物。不論以色列，希臘精神時代，羅馬文學白銀時代，或現代浪漫蒂克運動，均不例外。

　　這個都市的女郎，躱在家裏，看見她的愛人來找她，呼喚她跟他一同到郊外去，叫他們得以歌頌全美的春天（2：8—13）。

<blockquote>

我的愛人來了，聽！

他越山陟嶺。

我的愛人像隻羚羊或牡鹿；

看，他站在我們的牆後，

望戶牖，

窺窗櫺。

愛人對我說：

起來，心愛的嬌娃，往前行。

看啊，冬天過了，

雨水也停；

花兒吐豔遍大地，

這時節正好揚起歌聲，

四境聽得見斑鳩的歡鳴。

無花果結實靑靑，

葡萄蕊播送着淸馨。

起來，心愛的嬌娃，往前行。

</blockquote>

67

CHAPTER NINE

THE LOVER'S WELCOME

That a new song begins here seems clear. The beloved is here pictured as hiding among the cliffs, instead of being in her city home, and the lover calls upon her not to go out with him to the countryside, but to show herself to him. Her response is expressed cryptically. Little foxes have been devouring the vinyards already in bloom. Does she mean that young men have already found their way to her? (2:14-15).

THE LOVER: O my dove, in the clefts of the rock, in the

shadow of the cliff,

Let me see thy face, let me hear thy voice;

For sweet is thy voice, and thy face is comely.

THE BELOVED: The foxes have seized us, the little foxes that

spoil the vineyards;

For our vineyard is in blossom.

九　愛人的歡迎

這顯然是一首新歌的發端。吉士描繪他心愛的人兒不是住在城市的家裏，而是躲在縣崖絕壁裏。他要求他的愛人不必出來，和他到野外去，只要她露出芳姿。她的回答是用含蓄的說法。小狐狸把那正在開花的葡萄園摧殘了。她是否覺得那些少年人已找到抵達她那裏的路向了呢（2：14—15）？

> 吉士：我的鴿子，在磐石穴裏，
>
> 　　　在懸崖蔭中躲藏；
>
> 　　　願聽你令音，瞻你面龐；
>
> 　　　你的面龐秀美，令音將將。
>
> 靜女：狐狸搜索了我們，是那些
>
> 　　　搗毀葡萄園的小狐狸；
>
> 　　　因為我們的葡萄園正是花時。

CHAPTER TEN

SURRENDER

The maiden speaks of the love binding her and her lover, and invites him to taste the joys of love until dawn (2:16-17).

My beloved is mine, and I am his, who feeds among the lilies.
Until the day break, and the shadows flee,
Turn, my love, and be like a gazelle or a young hart
Upon the mountain of spices.

十　投降

　　女郎說到愛情把她和她的愛人固結在一起，邀請他嘗試愛情的滋味
直到天曉（2：16--17）。

> 愛人屬乎我，我屬我愛人，
>
> 他在百合花叢牧放。
>
> 等天色破曉，陰影歛藏，
>
> 囘轉，心愛的，像--隻麇鹿或羚羊，
>
> 在那芳菲的山岡。

CHAPTER ELEVEN
THE DREAM OF THE LOST LOVER

The pathos of love's separation is movingly described in this song. Dreaming of her absent lover, the beloved wanders through the streets seeking him, until she finds him and holds him fast. She too, like the happy maiden in 2:7, adjures the daughters of Jerusalem not to disturb their love—but her reunion with her lover is only in a dream. The repetition of those passion-charged words highlights the pathos of the lovers' separation.

The sorrowful echo of an imaginary fulfillment recalls the scene in Christopher Marlowe's play, "Dr. Faustus," when the hero, in the last few hours before the Devil comes to claim his soul, revelry, "O lente, lente, currite noctis equi," "O slowly, slowly, run revelry, "O lente, lente, currite notis equi," "O slowly, slowly, run on, ye coursers of the night" (3:1-5).

On my couch at night I sought him whom I love,
Sought him, but found him not.
"I will rise now, and go about the city,
On the streets and highways,
I will seek him whom I love."
I sought him, but I found him not.
The watchmen making their rounds in the **city found me.**
"Have you seen him, whom I love?"
Scarcely had I passed them,
When I found him whom I love.
I held him, and would not let him go,
Until I had brought him into my mother's **house,**
Into the chamber of her that conceived me.
"I adjure you, O daughters of Jerusalem,
By the gazelles, and by the hinds of the field,
That you disturb not, nor interrupt our love,
Until it be satiated."

十一 失愛者之夢

這詩述說出叫人傷懷的分離。夢想她離去的愛人，她蹬蹀街頭去尋覓，直到遇見他，就很緊地抓住他。她也像那快樂的女郎，懇求耶路撒冷衆女子，別打擾她們的好夢（2：7）——但她和愛人的重圓僅是一場夢。重温那熱情的懇求是愛人彼此乖隔的傷感的高潮。

一種空中樓閣的傷心同響，叫人憶起克里斯托帕馬老的戲劇「褒斯塔斯醫生」來，那英雄在魔鬼將召他的魂魄之前幾小時，由一個愛人當他狂歡之際複述奧維特的話：「慢些，慢些，按照次序地來，你們這些夜間的狩獵者」（3：1—5）。

> 夜間我在榻上尋覓情郎，
> 尋覓，卻不見他的影蹤，
> 現在我要起來，到城中，
> 向街上和康莊，
> 尋覓情郎。
> 尋覓，依舊不見他的影蹤。
> 戍卒巡邏時發現了我。
> 「你們可曾見到我的情郎？」
> 剛剛離開了他們，
> 就找到我的情郎。
> 我抓住他，不讓他去遊蕩，
> 帶他到我媽的內室，
> 到那孕育我者的臥房。
> 「我向你們呼籲，耶城的女子們，
> 指着田野間的羚羊與母鹿，
> 你們別攪擾，打斷我們的愛，
> 等到它滿足。」

CHAPTER TWELVE
A WEDDING SONG FOR SOLOMON

This song is the oldest datable unit in the collection. It was written to mark the ceremonies connected with King Solomon's marriage to a foreign princess, perhaps from Egypt, across the desert. Another example of a royal wedding hymn, not connected with Solomon, is to be found in Psalm 45. Here the arrival of the princess' elaborate entourage is described by the court poets (3:6-11).

Who is this coming from the wilderness,
Like thick clouds of smoke?
Perfumed with myrrh and frankincense,
With all powders of the merchant?
Behold, it is the litter of Solomon;
Sixty heroes round about it,
Of the heroes of Israel,
All skilled with the sword,
Expert in war.
Every man has his sword at his side
To ward off the terrors of the night.
A palanquin has the king made for himself,
Solomon, of Lebanon-wood.
He has made its pillars of silver,
Its inlay of gold,
Its seat of purple,
Its innermost parts being inlaid with ivory—
From the daughters of Jerusalem.
Go forth, O daughters of Zion,
And gaze upon King Solomon,
Arrayed in the crown with which his mother has crowned him
On his wedding-day,
On the day of his heart's gladness.

十二 所羅門結婚進行曲

這首詩可推算是最古老的片斷被收在樂裏。它描繪的是所羅門王和一位外國（或者是埃及）公主結親，迎親的行列從沙漠經過的情形。另一篇王室結婚進行曲的例子，和所羅門王無關，見於詩篇四十五篇。這裏佈置公主來臨時精巧的場面是宮庭詩人所描述的（3：6—11）。

是誰從野地來臨，
正像馫靡的煙雲？
用商人各種香粉
沒藥乳香來薰？
看，所羅門的舁牀，
六十個勇士護衞在旁，
都是以色列之強，
劍術精到，
跑慣戰場。
個個佩着寶刀，
好鎮壓夜裏的驚惶。
所羅門王爲自己造一乘轎子，
利巴嫩木做轎身，
柱子用純銀，
轎底鑲黃金，
坐墊紫黑色，
裏面鋪上象牙般的文茵——
出自耶城女子們的愛心。
趕上去，錫安的衆女郎，
瞻望所羅門王，
他在結婚的良辰
王母替他加冕多堂皇，
這一天他的心花眞怒放。

75

CHAPTER THIRTEEN
MY BELOVED IS PERFECT

A characteristic was.f in praise of the physical perfection of the beloved. Both the standard of feminine beauty that is extolled and the mode of expression that is employed are characteristic of the ancient Orient (4:1-7).

Thou art fair, my love, thou art fair!
Thine eyes are as doves behind thy veil,
Thy hair is as a flock of goats,
Streaming down from mount Gilead.
Thy teeth are like a flock ready for shearing,
Who have come from the washing,
All paired alike, and none missing among them.
Thy lips are like a scarlet thread
And thy mouth is comely;
Thy temples are like a slice of pomegranate,
Seen behind thy veil.
Thy neck is like the tower of David
Which is built as a landmark,
A thousand shields hanging upon it,
All the armour of the heroes.
Thy two breasts are like two fawns,
Twins of a gazelle,
Feeding among the lilies.
Until the day break
And the shadows flee,
I will get me to the mountain of myrrh,
And to the hill of frankincense.
Thou art all fair, my love;
And there is no blemish upon thee.

十三　全美的愛人

　　這首是歌頌愛人形式完美的典型褒歌。無論稱讚女性美的標準或表情方式的刻畫，都具古代東方人的特色（3：1—7）。

> 你俊美，我愛的，你俊美！
> 那雙像鴿子的眼兒在羅帕裏，
> 頭髮好比山羊羣，
> 由基列頂奔流到山底。
> 皓齒如一羣待剪毛的馴羊，
> 從水中洗淨而起，
> 成雙成對，沒有殘缺不齊。
> 唇是一圈緋紅的綫子
> 口吻真甜蜜；
> 兩顋顯似石榴片，
> 隱在綸巾底。
> 頸子是大衛的高臺，
> 蓋來做分界碑，
> 懸着一千個盾牌，
> 全體壯士們的兵器。
> 兩個乳房像小鹿，
> 原來是雙生的小麋，
> 在百合花叢齧食。
> 等到天色破曉，
> 陰翳飛馳，
> 我要置身沒藥山，
> 在乳香岡上棲息。
> 我愛的，你十全十美；
> 絕無一點瑕疵。

77

CHAPTER FOURTEEN

CALL FROM THE MOUNTAINS

*From the Lebanon mountain range at the northern extremity
of Israel comes the lover's call to his bride (4:8).*

With me from Lebanon, my bride,
With me from Lebanon shalt thou come.
Leap from the top of Amana,
From the top of Senir and Hermon,
From the dens of the lions,
From the mountains of the leopards.

十四　山岳的呼喚

從利巴嫩山峯，以色列北部的絕頂，那愛人向他的佳耦呼喚（4：8）。

我的新婦，跟我出利巴嫩，

你要來跟我出利巴嫩。

橫過阿瑪那之巔，

陟示耳爾和黑門的絕巘，

越過獅子窩裕裕，

和有豹子的峯巒。

CHAPTER FIFTEEN

LOVE'S ENCHANTMENT

The charm of the beloved has quite ravished her lover, who finds her presence more fragrant than wine and perfume, or the strong, clean smell of Lebanon's cedars, and her kisses sweeter than milk and honey. On the use of "sister" as a term of endearment in this song and succeeding ones (4:9-11).

Thou hast ravished my heart, my sister, my bride;

Thou hast ravished my heart with one of thine eyes,

With one bead of thy necklace.

How fair is thy love, my sister, my bride!

How much better thy love than wine!

And the smell of thine ointments than all perfumes!

Thy lips, O my bride, drop honey —

Honey and milk are under thy tongue;

And the smell of thy garments is like the smell of Lebanon.

十五、令人消魂的愛情

美人傾城傾國的容貌叫她的愛人神魂顛倒，他瞻視她的丰姿，叫陳酒和香精無味，利巴嫩香柏木的清芬也失色，她的口吻比乳與蜜更甜美。這首詩和底下的一首用「妹子」這名詞，涵蘊着可珍愛的滋味（4：9--11）。

> 我妹子，我新婦，你讓我神魂顛倒；
>
> 因你眼睛的眸子顛倒，
>
> 因你項圈的珠兒魂銷。
>
> 你的愛情多美，我妹子，我佳耦！
>
> 那份愛情勝過春醪多多，
>
> 你膏油的氣味壓服一切香料！
>
> 你的唇滴下蜜汁，我的新婦----
>
> 舌底凝着蜜和酥；
>
> 你那長袍有利巴嫩的香馥。

CHAPTER SIXTEEN

LOVE'S BARRIERS

In this dialogue, the lover praises the delectable qualities of his beloved, but complains that he finds her a closed garden, a sealed fountain. She responds by declaring that, on the contrary, she is a free-flowing fountain, and implies that her lover has been backward. She therefore calls upon the winds to waft her fragrance to him, that he may come and enjoy the fruit of his garden. He accepts her invitation with alacrity, and finally announces the joy of love's consummation (4:12-5:1).

THE LOVER: A closed garden is my sister, my bride;
A closed spring, a fountain sealed.
Thy branches are a garden of pomegranates,
With precious fruits,
Henna with nard,
Spikenard and saffron, cassia and cinnamon,
With all trees of frankincense;
Myrrh and aloes, with all the chief spices.

THE BELOVED: The fountain in my garden is a well of
living waters,
Flowing down from Lebanon.
Awake, O north wind;
And come, O south;
Blow upon my garden,
Let its spices flow out,
Let my lover come into his garden,
And eat its delightful fruits.

THE LOVER: I have come into my garden,
my sister, my bride;
I have gathered my myrrh with my spice;
Eaten my honeycomb with my honey;
Drunken my wine with my milk.

THE BELOVED: Eat, O my friend,
Drink, yea, drink abundantly of love.

82

十六 愛情的欄栅

這段對話裏，吉士讚稱美人可喜的特質，但埋怨她像一個關鎖的園圃，閉塞的泉源。她回答時用反襯法宣布自己是一道自由湧流的泉源，暗示她的愛人太不靈敏。她因此呼喚風兒來吹出她的香味給他，讓他會進園中來饕用那些佳果。他快活地接受她的邀請，最後發表愛情高潮的樂趣（4：12—5：1）。

> 吉士：我妹子，我佳耦，
> 　　　　是個關鎖園；
> 　　　　是個封閉的靈源，禁錮的水泉。
> 　　　　你的柔條是滿園的石榴，
> 　　　　佳果纍纍色鮮妍，
> 　　　　又有哪噠與鳳仙，
> 　　　　松香，番紅花，桂樹，
> 　　　　各樣的乳香在吐豔，
> 　　　　沒藥，蘆薈和一切香草盡歡然。
> 靜女：我園裏那源泉是口活水井，
> 　　　　從利巴嫩滔滔下注。
> 　　　　醒起罷，北風，
> 　　　　惠臨罷，南風；
> 　　　　吹進我的園圃，
> 　　　　播送它的香味，
> 　　　　願我的愛人入他的苑囿，
> 　　　　從它的佳果得飽飫。
> 吉士：我進了我的園圃，我妹子，我伴耦；
> 　　　　採了我的沒藥和香草，
> 　　　　喫了我的蜂房和蜂蜜；
> 　　　　喝了我的乳汁和春醪。
> 靜女：喫罷，我的良友，
> 　　　　喝罷，啊，酣飲愛情當美酒。

83

CHAPTER SEVENTEEN
LOVE'S TRIAL AND TRIUMPH

The longest and most elaborate song in the collection takes the form of a dream-song. Within its framework, other patterns like the search for the absent lover and the was.f praising his person, are skillfully interwoven.

The song reflects the sophistication ana coquetry of the city maiden, whose artifices fall away before the power of love. The maiden is asleep, and in the dream she hears her lover knocking, begging to be admitted. She playfully answers that she has already retired for the night. Instead of continuing the badinage, as she expected, he leaves her doorway. Yearning for the sound of his voice, she runs out into the city streets, seeking for him everywhere. The city watchmen, mistaking her for a streetwalker, beat and wound her. She turns to the daughters of Jerusalem — everything is possible in a dream — and begs them to tell her lover that she is lovesick for him. How can they distinguish her lover from all others? Triumphantly she answers that he is unique for beauty, strength and charm. Impressed with her description, the daughters of Jerusalem offer to help find him. The maiden, however, feels that discretion is much the better part, and that too much help from them may be dangerous to her cause. She disclaims their assistance and joyously announces that her lover has already found his way to his garden. He is hers alone, and she is his (5:2 — 6:3).

I was asleep, but my heart was awake.
Hark! my love is knocking:
"Open to me, my sister, my love, my dove, my perfect one,
For my head is filled with dew,
My locks, with the drops of the night."
"I have already put off my coat,
Why should I put it on again;
I have washed my feet,
Why should I soil them?"
My beloved withdrew his hand from the door's opening,
And my heart was stirred for him.

十七　愛情的苦樂

　　這是集中最長而刻意經營的一首，是採用做夢的形式。它的體制，和前面尋覓看不見的情人和讚美他的儀表的褒歌的模型，一樣有巧妙的組織。

　　這歌反映出一個辯才無礙，善於撒嬌的城市女郎，她的手段鬥不過愛情的權力。這女郎是在睡鄉裏，聽見愛人在敲門，要求進入屋裏。她戲謔地回答他，說她自己已經上牀休息了。代替着繼續的調侃，正像她所期望的，他離開她的門檻。她戀念他的聲音，跑到城中的街上，處處去尋找他。巡邏的兵卒誤認她是遊蕩者，把她打傷了。她轉向耶路撒冷的女子們——一切的事在夢裏都是可能的——懇求她們告訴她的愛人，說她思念到生病。她的愛人要怎樣識別呢？她意氣高揚地回答着，說她的愛人是漂亮絕倫，剛強與迷人。耶路撒冷的女子們因她述說的感動，答應要幫她的忙。但這女郎覺得最好還是謹慎一些，因為從她們得了太多的援助是會誤事的。她拒絕了她們的幫忙，並快樂地宣佈她的愛人已經找到進他園中的路向。他惟獨屬乎她，而她也是屬乎他的(5：2—6：3)。

　　　　　　我睡了，內心卻醒覺。
　　　　　　聽！愛人在叩門：
　　　　　　「替我開，我妹妹，我愛的，我鴿子，我完人，
　　　　　　我的腦袋溼了，
　　　　　　我的頭髮爲夜露所霑。」
　　　　　　「我已經脫了外套，
　　　　　　再穿上怎能夠；
　　　　　　我已經洗了雙腳，
　　　　　　叫它們再髒掉？」
　　　　　　愛人從鑰隙縮回了手，
　　　　　　我的心爲他而窘擾。
　　　　　　我起來替愛人開門，

85

I rose to open to my beloved,
And my hands were dripping with myrrh,
My fingers, with flowing myrrh,
Upon the handles of the bar.
I opened to my beloved,
But my beloved was gone and away.
My soul longed for his word;
I sought him, but could not find him;
I called him, but he gave me no answer.
The watchmen going about the city found me,
They struck me, they wounded me,
The keepers of the walls stripped my mantle from me.
"I adjure you, O daughters of Jerusalem,
If ye find my beloved,
What shall you tell him?
That I am faint with love."
"What is thy lover more than any other,
O fairest among women?
What is thy lover more than any other,
That thou dost so adjure us?"
"My beloved is fair and ruddy,
Pre-eminent above ten thousand.
His head is the finest gold,
His locks are curled, black as a raven.
His eyes are like doves, beside the water-brooks,
Bathing in milk, sitting at a brimming pool.
His cheeks are as beds of spices,

我的手滴下沒藥，
指頭溢出沒藥津，
把門閂弄得溼淋淋。
我替愛人開了門，
愛人卻走得無影無蹤。
我的魂戀慕他的詞鋒；
我找他，徒勞無功，
我喊他，他像是耳聾。
邏卒巡城時遇見我，
打我，我受了傷，
守城人奪去我的斗篷。
「耶城的女子們，我求你們：
如碰見我的愛人，
你們要怎樣向他指陳？
為了愛我耗盡了精神。」
「你所愛的有甚麼過人的地方，
噢！你這最美的女郎？
你所愛的有甚麼過人的地方，
才這樣央求我們幫忙？」
「我的愛人英俊又殷紅，
萬人比不上他的高風。
他的腦袋是精金
他的頭髮鬈曲，黑得像慈烏那麼沈。
眼睛像溪水旁的鴿子，
在乳汁中洗濯，坐在水潯。
他的雙頰是芳草畦
逸出了香氣，

Exuding perfumes,
His lips are as lilies,
That drop with flowing myrrh.
His arms are rods of gold
Set with beryl,
His body is a column of ivory,
Overlaid with sapphires.
His legs are pillars of marble,
Set upon sockets of fine gold,
His appearance is like Lebanon,
Lordly as the cedars.
His mouth is sweetness itself,
He is altogether a delight.
This is my beloved, and this is my friend,
O daughters of Jerusalem."
"Where is thy lover gone,
O fairest among women?
Where has thy lover turned,
That we may seek him with thee?"
"My beloved is gone down to his garden,
To the beds of spices,
To feed in the gardens,
And to gather lilies.
I am my lover's,
And my beloved is mine,
As he feeds among the lilies."

他的嘴唇是百合花，
滴下了沒藥液。
他的膀臂像金管
嵌上了白玉
他的軀幹是象牙軸，
鑲了藍寶石。
他的脛是大理石雕成的，
放上精金座，
他的儀容像利巴嫩，
風度勝過香柏樹。
他的嘴巴那麼甜，
全然惹人的愛慕。
耶路撒冷的女子們，
這就是我的朋友，我的情侶。」
「你的愛人到那裏，
你這女子中最美的？
你的愛人轉向何方，
我們好去尋找幫你忙？」
「我的愛人下到他的園中，
進入香草圃，
在苑中牧羧，
採摘百合花朶朶。
我屬我愛人，
愛人屬乎我，
他倚偎百合花和羣羊為伍。」

CHAPTER EIGHTEEN
THE POWER OF BEAUTY

This is a very old was.f, which can be dated during the first half-century of the Divided Kingdom (between 930 and 880 B. C. E.). The lover praises his beloved's beauty, by comparing her to the two capitals of the country, Jerusalem in the south and Tirzah in the north. The repetition of several phrases that are familiar to us from earlier songs in the collection is natural in popular poetry (6:4-7).

Thou art beautiful, O my love, as Tirzah,

Comely as Jerusalem,

Awe-inspiring as these great sights!

Turn thine eyes away from me,

For they have overcome me.

Thy hair is as a flock of goats,

Streaming down from Gilead.

Thy teeth are like a flock of ewes,

Who have come up from the washing;

All paired alike and none missing among them.

Thy temple is a slice of pomegranate

Seen behind thy veil.

十八　美的魔力

這是一首最古老的褒歌，可斷定是王國分裂的上半世紀的產品（主前930和880）。吉士稱讚他那情侶的美貌，是用南方的耶路撒冷，北方的得撒，這兩個都會去比儗她。許多反覆重述的短語，對於我們並不陌生，因集中較早的詩歌已經用過，是大眾詩歌的本色（6：4－7）。

> 我愛的，你像得撒的瑰逸，
> 像耶路撒冷般挺秀，
> 這壯闊的景象叫人呆住！
> 請你把眼睛轉離我
> 因它們叫我迷惘。
> 你的頭髮好比山羊羣
> 從基列滾流而下，勢滃泱。
> 你的牙齒如一羣母羊，
> 洗完浴由水而上；
> 兩兩成雙，無一失喪。
> 你的頰顴似石榴切片，
> 隱在帕子裏面。

CHAPTER NINETEEN

THE ONE AND ONLY

The lover has heard of the resplendent ladies in the royal court, but for him there is only one, unique and perfect, the favorite even of her mother among all her children. No wonder all women unite in praising her (6:8-9).

There are threescore queens,

And fourscore concubines,

And maidens without number.

But my dove, my pure one, is one alone,

The only one for her mother,

The choice of her that bore her.

Maidens saw her, and called her happy,

Even queens and concubines, and they praised her.

十九　獨一無二

那吉士聽見有許多光華煥發的婦女在宮庭裏，但他所愛的只有一人，完美無倫，在她母親所生的她最得寵。莫怪所有的婦女都一齊來讚美她（C：8—9）。

那裏有六十個后妃，
八十個宮婦，
還有童女無數。
但我的鴿子，我的淑女，只有一人，
是她母親最寵惜的嬌兒，
生她的，愛她如掌珍。
衆女見了她，說她眞快樂，
后妃與宮婦也稱道她的幸福。

CHAPTER TWENTY

LOVE'S DAWNING

For the lover, the beauty of the maiden can only be compared to the hosts of heaven. Spring is here, and he resolves to go down to his garden, to see the fruit-trees in blossom. There his beloved will let him enjoy her fragrance.

The last verse is incomprehensible in the accepted text (6:10-12).

Who is she gazing forth like the morning star,

Fair as the moon,

Bright as the sun,

Awe-inspiring like these great sights?

I have come into the garden of nuts,

To look at the tender shoots of the valley,

To see whether the vine has budded,

And the pomegranates are in flower.

I am beside myself with joy,

For there thou wilt give me thy myrrh,

O noble kinsman's daughter!

二十　愛情的曙光

在吉士眼裏，那靜女的容輝惟有天上的衆辰可以媲美。春天來了，他決定下園圃去，觀賞果樹在萌發。在那裏心愛的靜女要把她的芬芳獻給他享用。

在大衆所接受的板本中，最後一節是無從索解的，（我根據歌底斯的修訂加以改譯）（6：10─12）。

> 她是誰，看來像晨星，
> 像月亮的秀麗和平，
> 像太陽的煥彩光明，
> 這樣壯闊的景象叫人震驚？
> 我進到核桃圃，
> 觀賞嫩綠的澤藪，
> 看葡萄萌芽沒有，
> 石榴開花與否。
> 我眞會得意忘形，
> 在那裏你要贈我以沒藥，馥又香，
> 噢，貴戚的女郎！

CHAPTER TWENTY ONE

THE MAIDEN'S DANCE

Among the Syrian peasants in our time, it is customary for the bride to perform a sword-dance on her wedding day. Our song has often been regarded as a Hebrew counterpart of this Syrian practice. This may well be the case, since the "king," or bridegroom, is mentioned in the song, though there is no reference to a sword in our text. What is certain is that the maiden is dancing, revealing both her grace of movement and her physical charms. She is referred to as the maid of Shulem, after a town (Biblical Shunem, modern Arabic, Sulem) which was famous for its beautiful women. This epithet "Shulammite" in Hebrew was mistaken for the proper name of a rustic maiden with whom Solomon fell in love.

The song begins with the company's call to her to turn, so that her comeliness may be observed. She modestly wonders what they can see in her. They proceed, however, to describe the beauty of her body in motion, from her dancing feet to the crowning glory of her tresses (7:1-6).

THE COMPANY: "Turn, turn, O maid of Shulem,
Turn, turn, so that we can see thee!"

THE MAIDEN: "What will you see in the maid of Shulem?"

THE COMPANY: "Indeed, the counter-dance!

How beautiful are thy steps in sandals,
O nobleman's daughter!

The roundings of thy thighs are
like jewelled links,

The handiwork of a craftsman.

96

廿一　女郎的舞姿

在我們的時代敘利亞的農民有這種風俗，新娘在結婚那一天要表演劍舞。雅歌常被認爲希伯來人具有敘利亞人這種習尚的佐證。本段該是指這件事的。所謂「王」或新郎，在歌中被提出，只是這段沒有指明帶着劍。但我們可以確信那女郎是在舞蹈，顯示她靈雅的動作和優美的體格。歌中指出她是書念的女郎，這個市鎮以產美女著稱。這綽號叫「書拉麥女郎」的在希伯來文被誤會爲所羅門所鍾愛的村女的特有名稱。

詩歌從她的友伴呼喚她囘轉而開始，她們欣賞她妙曼的姿態。她謙謹地問她們能够從自己看到甚麼。接着，她們描摹她的軀體在運動中的美姿，由跳躍的脚談到戴着堂皇冠冕的髮鬌（7：1—6）。

友伴：「轉，轉過來，書念女郎，

　　　　轉，轉過來，我們好欣賞你的容光！」

女郎：「你們會從書念女郎看到什麼呢？」

友伴：「高貴的女子，

　　　　眞的，向後舞蹈！

　　　　你著鞋的蓮步多美好！

　　　　你那圓腿像玉環，

　　　　經過巧工的雕刓。

97

Thy naval is like a round goblet
In which the wine-mixture is not lacking.
Thy belly is like a heap of wheat,
Set about with lilies.
Thy two breasts are like two fawns,
Twins of a gazelle.
Thy neck is as a tower of ivory.
Thine eyes are pools in Heshbon,
At the gate of Bath-rabbim,
Thy nose is like the tower of Lebanon
Facing toward Damascus.
Thy head upon thee is like crimson,
And the hair of thy head like purple—
A king is held captive in its tresses!"

不缺少調和的酒，
你肚臍像玉杯般渾圓•
你的腰是小麥堆，
安放在百合花之間。
兩乳似一對麋鹿
是母鹿的孿生子。
頸子好比象牙臺。
兩眼兒像希實本的水池，
坐落巴拉賓門外，
鼻梁宛然利巴嫩塔
朝向大馬斯礒。
你的頭的顏色殷紅，
頭髮的顏色深紫，
王受那些髮綹所糾住！」

CHAPTER TWENTY TWO

HOW DELIGHTFUL IS LOVE

In this rhapsody to love, the lover compares his chosen one to a slender and stately palm-tree and announces his intention of climbing up its branches and enjoying its delights (7:7-10).

The succeeding verses (7:11-14) may possibly constitute the beloved's reply. Since, however, our passage is not a plea directly addressed to the beloved, but rather a song of praise, and the next verses are not couched as a reply, it seems likelier that we have two independent songs here.

How fair and how pleasant art thou, love, with its delights!

Thy form is like a palm-tree,

Thy breasts, like clusters of grapes.

I said: "I will climb up into my palm-tree,

And take hold of its branches.

Let thy breasts be as clusters of the vine,

And the fragrance of thy face like apples,

For thy kiss is like the finest wine

That gives power to lovers,

And stirs the lips of the sleepers with desire."

廿二 多麼可喜的愛情

在這首愛情的狂想曲中。吉士把他所選中的情人比作纖小莊嚴的棕樹，並宣佈他要爬上它的枝子，享受它的樂趣（7：7—10）。

下面幾節的歌詞（7：11—14）可能構成靜女的答詞。這首的章句既然不是向他的愛人直接發表的懇求，而是一種褒歌，接上來的自非一種答案，看來好像是兩首獨立的詩歌。

愛人，你多美貌，多惹人愛，叫人喜悅！

你的身段像一株棕樹亭亭玉立。

兩乳像纍纍的葡萄眞堪採摘。

我說：「我要爬上我的棕樹，

握住它的枝。

你乳房是葡萄纍纍下垂，

你的臉有蘋果的芳馡。

因你的香吻勝佳釀，

能給愛人以力量，

用渴慕把入夢者的嘴唇攪動。」

CHAPTER TWENTY THREE

THE BELOVED'S PROMISE

*With a joyous affirmation of the love binding her and her
lover, the maiden calls upon him to come out into the fields and
vineyards, blooming in the glory of the spring. There, she promises,
she will give him her love (7:11-14).*

I am my beloved's,

And for me is his desire.

Come, my beloved, let us go forth into the field,

Let us lodge among the villages,

And rise early for the vineyards.

Let us see whether the vine has budded,

Whether the vine-blossom has opened,

And the pomegranates have flowered —

There will I give thee my love.

The mandrakes are giving forth their fragrance,

And at our door are all sweet fruits,

Both new and old —

There will I give thee my love,

Which I have laid up for thee.

廿三　靜女的諾言

靜女喜悅地保證把她和吉士用愛情連繫在一起，靜女呼喚他出門到田野間及葡萄園去，和春天的花爭榮。她答應在那裏要把那份愛情獻給他（7：11—14）。

我屬我愛人，
他給我的是他的渴慕。
來，我愛人，我們一同到田野去，
我們在村莊裏投宿，
好早點起身進葡萄圃。
看葡萄可曾萌芽
葡萄的新苞可曾開過，
石榴渥花與否——
在那兒我要獻上愛情給您享受。
蔓陀羅放出芳馥，
我們的門庭裏有各種佳果，
新的舊的——
在那兒我要贈您以愛情，
這是我特地爲您留住。

CHAPTER TWENTY FOUR

WOULD THOU WERT MY BROTHER

The maiden has been exposed to the taunts of neighbors and friends, when she has given public expression to her love. If only her lover were her foster-brother, raised in the same home! None could reproach her, then, if she were to kiss him in the street, lead him to her mother's home and drink wine at his side. In her reverie, she pictures the bliss in her lover's company, and calls upon the daughters of Jerusalem not to disturb her imagined ecstasy (8:1-4).

Would thou wert indeed my brother,

Who had suckled at my mother's breasts!

If I found thee outside, I could kiss thee;

Yet no one would despise me.

I would bring thee to my mother's house

Who had taught me,

I would give thee spiced wine to drink

The juice of pomegranates.

His left hand would be beneath my head,

And his right hand would embrace me.

And I would exclaim,

"I adjure you, O daughters of Jerusalem:

Why should you disturb or interrupt our love

Until it be satiated?"

廿四　若你是我的兄弟

女郎向她的愛人公然揭示愛情，遭受鄰舍和朋友的嘲笑。如果她的愛人是她同養的兄弟，在她家裏孕育長大！苟她在街上吻他，領他進母親的住宅，在他身伴喝酒，總沒有人敢非難她。在她的幻想中，描繪自己在愛人的友伴中的寵遇，而呼籲耶路撒冷衆女子不要打擾她想像中的歡樂（8：1—4）。

如果您眞地是我的兄弟，
曾在我母親胸懷哺乳！
我若在外邊找到您，可以吻您；
沒有人敢相輕侮。
我要領您進我母親的屋裏
她曾教導我，
要請您喝香醪，
就是石榴漿。
他的左手放在我頭下，
他的右手把我攬住。
我要揚聲，
「耶城的女子們，我向你們呼籲：
爲甚麼要攪擾，打斷我們的愛，
不讓它滿足？」

CHAPTER TWENTY FIVE
LOVE UNDER THE APPLE-TREE

This passage, which may be fragmentary, is not very clear, principally because of the symbolism employed. It seems to be a duet, where the company greets the advent of the maiden leaning on her lover. She, however, has no ear for their words, but addresses her lover. She reminds him that she woke him from his sleep under the apple-tree. It was at the self-same spot that he had come into the world, because of the love of his father and mother. The apple-tree, a familiar erotic symbol, is, as Jastrow notes, the sexual passion which passes from one generation to the next. The maiden is apparently calling him to respond to her love (8:5).

THE COMPANY: Who is this coming up from the wilderness,
                       Clinging to her beloved?

THE BELOVED: Under the apple-tree I woke thee,
                       There thy mother gave thee birth,
                       Yea, there she who bore thee brought thee
                         forth.

廿五　蘋果樹下之戀

這段或者是殘闕不全的，不很清晰，主要的是因爲它使用象徵的手法。看來像是對白，在那邊友伴們因女郎依傍着她的愛人來臨而歡暢。但她卻不睬他們，顧自和愛人交談。她重提曾在蘋果樹下叫醒他。他就是在那地方出世的，是他父母之愛的結晶。蘋果樹，一種熟悉的性愛的象徵，依賈士突羅的註釋：性愛的藝術是一代傳遞給一代的。女郎顯然地呼籲他以愛相報（8：5）。

友伴：伊誰從野地而上，

　　　　側身倚偎她的情郎？

女郎：在蘋果樹底下，我把你催醒，

　　　　你媽在那兒產下嬌嬰，

　　　　是的，那懷你胎的在那兒讓你誕生。

CHAPTER TWENTY SIX

THE SEAL OF LOVE

The maiden can not bear any separation from her lover. She therefore pleads to be as close to him as his seal. The ancients carried their seals either as a ring on the finger or as a necklace near the heart.

The frank and unabashed avowal of love throughout the book reaches its impressive climax here where it is described as a mighty force, the very flame of God. Thus the basic truth underlying the Song of Songs is emphasized, that natural love is holy (8:6-7).

Set me as a seal upon thy heart,

As a seal upon thine arm,

For love is strong as death,

Passion is unyielding as the grave.

Its flashes are flashes of fire,

A flame of God.

Many waters can not extinguish love,

Nor can the floods sweep it away.

If a man gave all the wealth of his house

In exchange for love,

He would be laughed to scorn.

廿六　愛的烙印

　　女郞受不了和愛人分離的痛苦。因此她懇求要和他密合得像他的烙印一般。古代的烙印好像指上的指戒和心窩旁邊垂着的項鍊一般。

　　坦率不畏蒽地表露愛情的作風，充塞全書，到這裏已達最高潮的記號，愛被描繪爲--種可怕的能力，上帝的烈燄。雅歌所强調的完全基於這種觀點，性愛是神聖的（8：6—7）。

　　　　　　把我鐫刻在心上作符信，
　　　　　　敝烺在臂上當烙印，
　　　　　　愛情頑强好比催命符，
　　　　　　慾火難制活像幽壤刃。
　　　　　　煌煌是雷鞭，
　　　　　　上帝的烈燄。
　　　　　　愛情，衆水滅不了，
　　　　　　洪流沖不散。
　　　　　　有誰想用全家的財產
　　　　　　去換取愛情，
　　　　　　一定遭受譏笑與厭賤。

CHAPTER TWENTY SEVEN

THE RAMPARTS OF LOVE

The young maiden is surrounded by suitors who complain that she is not ready for love and marriage. Their determination to break down her resistance they express by using the formula of an oath. If she remains obdurate, like the wall of a city, they will lay siege to her. This they plan to do in approved military fashion, by building around her another temporary embankment, from which they will launch the "attack." That their intentions are not hostile is clear from the materiel of war that they intend to employ in their campaign, silver and cedar-wood. These expensive goods probably symbolize the gifts that they are showering upon her.

She answers that she is indeed like a wall, impregnable to their importunities, but not because she is too young for love. On the contrary, she is ready for the great experience, but only with him whom she loves and strives to please above all others (8:8-10).

THE SUITORS: We have a little sister,

But she has no breasts.

What shall we do with our sister,

On this day when she is being spoken for?

If she be a wall,

We will build a turret of silver against her;

If she be a gate,

We will besiege her with boards of cedar.

THE MAIDEN: I am a wall,

And my breasts are like towers,

Therefore am I in my lover's eyes

As one finding favor.

廿七　愛情的堅壘

一個年青的女郎遭受求婚者的包圍，他們抱怨她還沒有作戀愛和婚姻的準備。他們決定要衝破她的防禦，用一種誓言的方式申明。若她繼續冷酷無情，像城牆一樣，他們要加以圍攻。他們計劃要用公認的軍事型式，藉着築造另一個暫時的戰壕圍繞她，從那裏發動「攻勢」。他們所要使用以攻擊的武器的質地是銀和香柏木，可見他們並沒有敵視的意向。這些奢侈品或者是他們呈示給她的象徵性的禮物。

她回答說自己真像一座城，不會因他們強求而陷落，也不是她年紀太小不合於談情說愛。相反地，她已準備好要領畧那奇妙的滋味，惟只願和她所愛的共享，並力求其喜悅，超過一切其他的人（8：8－10）。

> 求婚者：我們有個小妹子，
> 　　　　她還沒有高聳的乳峯。
> 　　　　當人來議婚的日子，
> 　　　　我們將何所適從？
> 　　　　如果她是一座城，
> 　　　　我們要造銀梁麗去衝撞，
> 　　　　如果她是一重門，
> 　　　　我們要用香柏盾去圍攻。
> 女郎：我是一座城，
> 　　　我的雙乳是樓臺，
> 　　　我在情郎眼裏，
> 　　　是邀寵的乖乖。

CHAPTER TWENTY EIGHT

THE FINEST VINEYARD

The genuine joys of love are graphically contrasted with the illusory satisfactions of wealth. The lover recalls that King Solomon owned a large and fruitful vineyard containing a thousand vines. It was worked by tenant-farmers, who received one-fifth of the income for their labor. The lover may be poor in money, yet he is far richer than Solomon, for he possesses a priceless treasure, the vineyard of his beloved (8:11-12).

Solomon owned a vineyard at Baal Hamon

Which he gave over to tenants.

For its fruit one would give

A thousand pieces of silver.

But my vineyard, my very own, is before me.

You, Solomon, are welcome to your thousand,

And your vine-tenders to their two hundred!

廿八　最美的葡萄園

　　愛情眞正的快樂和財富虚幻的滿足在此作一寫實的對照。那情郎憶起所羅門王有一個大而繁榮的葡萄園，培植了一千株的葡萄樹。交佃農經管，他們可得總收入五分之一爲工資。這個情郎在經濟上講，或者不豐裕；實際上卻遠比所羅門富有，因他擁有無價之寶——她愛人的葡萄園（8：11—12）。

　　　　所羅門有個葡萄園
　　　　在巴愛爾哈門，
　　　　他把它交給農人。
　　　　爲着它的果子
　　　　人須付上一千兩銀。
　　　　但在我面前有屬乎我
　　　　爲我而設的葡萄園。
　　　　所羅門，你盡管得你那一千，
　　　　你的園丁也得兩百員。

CHAPTER TWENTY NINE

LET ME HEAR THY VOICE

The beloved, sitting in the garden, is surrounded by her companions. Her lover pleads with her to invite him to enjoy the delights of love. As he quotes the words that he wishes to hear her say, he employs the familiar figures of the soung deer and the fragrant mountain to symbolize the lover and his beloved (8:13-14).

Thou dwelling amid the gardens,

While thy companions are listening,

Let me hear thy voice, saying to me,

"Make haste, my beloved,

And be like a gazelle or a young hart

Upon the mountains of spices."

廿九　讓我聽到你的聲音

那靜女坐在園裏，她的友伴圍繞在她周遭。她的情郎請求她邀他去享受愛情的愉樂。當他引她的話——他所期望聽見的，使用熟悉的標誌——小鹿和香草山，以象徵情郎和他的愛侶（8：13—14）。

> 你住在園裏，
> 你的友伴在諦聽，
> 讓我得聆你的柔聲，對我說：
> 「快些，我的情郎，
> 您得像小鹿或羚羊，
> 在那香草的山岡。」

良人轉身去　啓戶空迎迓
呼之無同音　覓之不見駕

農下核桃園　谷中察蕃蔚

葡萄萌芽否　石榴開花未

The Song of Solomon

CHAPTER ONE

The Song of Songs, which is Solomon's
O that you would kiss me
    with the kisses of your mouth!
For your love s better than wine,

Your anointing oils are fragrant,
Your name is oil poured out;
    Therefore the maidens love you.

Draw me after you, let us make haste.
    The king has brought me into his chambers.
We will exult and rejoice in you;
    We will extol your love more than wine;
    Rightly do they love you.

I am very dark, but comely,
    O daughters of Jerusalem,
Like the tents of Kedar,
    Like the curtains of Solomon.

Do not gaze at me because I am swarthy,
    Because the sun has scorched me.
My mother's sons were angry with me,
    They made me keeper of the vineyards;
    But, my own vineyard I have not kept!

第一首

所羅門之歌

寵儂以甜吻
子名如膏油
眾花自羨日

顧子引儂惱
君王攜子廷
戎儕因之喜
激賞子慕嬡
群花爭子慕

郁城諸佚女
儂膚雛黛昊
妁基達銀幕

莫同強
輕母儂
黑仲圍

歌中之雅歌

愛情美瓊漿
傾倒溢馨香
童女慕高風

形影時相將
攜儂入椒房
此樂難計量
勝舉玉液觴
眩眼萬丈光

請聽儂陳辭
獨蘊絕世姿
儼羅門朱帷

嬌然葡萄園
鮮念自灼日
園萄萄波守

Tell me, you whom my soul loves,

    Where you pasture your flock,

    Where you make it lie down at noon;

For why should I be like one who wanders

    Besides the flocks of your companions?

If you do not know,

    O fairest among women,

Follow in the tracks of the flock,

    And pasture your kids

    Beside the shepherd's tents.

I compare you, my love,

    To a mare of Pharaoh's chariots.

Your cheeks are comely with ornaments,

    Your neck with strings of jewels.

We will make you ornaments of gold,

    Studded with silver.

While the king was on his couch,

    My nard gave forth its fragrance,

儂心所慕兮，牧羊在何許，
亭午憩何方，曷不發一語，
君不見儂在，友羊群旁佇。

咨爾絕色姝，蹦踱隅一駒，
蔄隨羣羊去，珈相至不棚，
寄放山羔羔，牧棚之一隅，
無為野卸牧。

佳耦何所似，法老車前駒。

兩顋因簪珥，秀色倍豐腴，
延頸何高華，高華繞串珠。

為爾挿金鈿，鑲銀以耀軀。

王方就座象牙榻，
儂之哪噠氣悠揚。

My beloved is to me a bag of myrrth,

That lies between my breasts.

My beloved is to me

A cluster of henna blossoms

In the vineyards of Enge'di.

Behold, you are beautiful, my love;

Behold, you are beautiful;

Your eyes are doves.

Behold, you are beautiful, my beloved;

Truly lovely.

Our couch is green;

The beams of our house are cedar,

Our rafters are pine.

君在儂眼裏　似一没藥囊
緊貼儂胸脯　時時吐芬芳

一棵鳳仙花　尤肖儂所親
屹立隱基底　葡園自生春

余之佳偶兮
爾至美
爾至美
明眸似鴿子

良人絶俊邁　倜儻若謫仙

青草為牀榻　郎儂好甜眠
香柏作屋棟　松樹以為椽

CHAPTER TWO

I am a rose of Sharon,
A lily of the valleys.

As a lily among brambles,
So is my love abong maidens.

As an apple tree
Among the trees of the wood,
So is my beloved
Among young men.
With great delight
I sat in his shadow,
And his fruit
Was sweet to my taste.

He brought me
To the banqueting house,
And his banner over me was love.

Sustain me with raisins,
Refresh me with apples;
For I am sick with love.

O that his left hand
Were under my head,
And that his right hand embraced me!

第二章

余乃沙崙野，百合榮華相。
花窪玫瑰山，特豪獨絕幽。

百合雛榮美，佳偶棄粉黛。
鄰今赫與荊，古與絕竟曠。

蘋果雜眾林，世下碩果頤。
良人生濁世，波清其陰嘗。
盒沈尋湛，精浮霧味。
垂俗行滋，匕與樂鮮，累不此色。

携儂延宴所，愛旗覆春陰。

葡乾增儂力，思慕轉成病。
蘋果快儂心，熱情難自禁。

左手為儂枕，右攏背至襟。

第二行有版本作「清逸白蓮苕」

125

I adjure you, O daughters of Jerusalem,
By the gazelles
Or the hinds of the field,
That you stir not up nor awaken love
Until it please.

The voice of my beloved!
Behold, he comes,

Leaping upon the mountains,
Bounding over the hills.

My beloved is like a gazelle,
Or a young stag.
Behold, there he stands
Behind our wall,
Gazing in at the windows,
Looking through the lattice.

My beloved speaks and says to me:
"Arise, my love, my fair one,
And come away;

For lo, the winter is past,
The rain is over and gone.

The flowers appear on the earth,
The time of singing has come,
And the voice of the turtledove
Is heard in our land.

郇城眾女兮
羚羊深山躚
毋令落荒芳
郎儂方繾綣

諦聽余叮嚀
毋廞郊外行
毋使夢中驚
欲飽飫春情

音聲峻嶺
人諸哀陵
是既

林偯尋
叢風所
出曉方
麀牖如
麋戶默

臨岑
來豋
已眾
與越
獧又

覺後窗櫺內
醒望牆窗戶
立視窗
羚羊方
小窺

良人懃告
　我愛卿
武美人
恕与余同行

殘冬已消逝　　春和時雨晴

大地萬苣放　　林間眾鳥鳴
方葺葡萄圍　　乍聆斑鳩聲

The fig tree puts forth its figs,

And the vines are in blossom;

They give forth fragrance.

Arise, my love, my fair one,

And come away.

O my dove, in the clefts of the rock,

In the covert of the cliff,

Let me see your face,

Let me hear your voice,

For your voice is sweet,

And your face is comely.

Catch us the foxes,

The little foxes,

That spoil the vineyards,

For our vineyards are in blossom."

My beloved is mine and I am his,

He pastures his flock among the lilies.

Until the day breathes

And the shadows flee,

Turn, my beloved, be like a gazelle,

Or a young stag

Upon rugged mountains.

生香，蕊卿。

葡萄愛行，葡萄我同。
寶人與余，結美人想，
果人、苓我、無。

螢熒鶯明，為之啼光，
石子效殊，以磐瞻我貌，容為玉。
子豪霰囀，分密密百，
鴿隱隱嬌，余之巖岩啼，陸陸鶯。

壞怪毀妖，來小擒此，
狐擒、狸貍，開園丁，正麗眾界，葡萄咨。

良人許，我何綴綠茵，
我屬良人，屬乎牧羊，
我在綴，良人、尻人、百合、苓叢。

飛歸菲，翳所偎芳，
雲知委，斂遊躑躅，煙遨躅。
天際羚羊上麂，越猶山峨，
風人清良，嵯峨。

CHAPTER THREE

Upon my bed by night
    I sought him whom my soul loves;
I sought him, but found him not;
    I called him, but he gave no answer.

"I will rise now and go about the city,
    In the streets and in the squares;
I will seek him whom my soul loves."
    I sought him, but found him not.

The watchmen found me,
    As they went about in the city.
"Have you seen him whom my soul loves?"

Scarcely had I passed them,
    When I found him whom my soul loves.
I held him, and would not let him go
    Until I had brought him
        into my mother's house,
    And into the chamber
        of her that conceived me.

I adjure you, O daughters of Jerusalem,
    By the gazelles
        or the hinds of the field,
That you stir not up nor awaken love
    Until it please.

第 三 首

思癡知
所徨我
求徒莫
寢心怛
窘寸忉

中鍾跤
城所覓
夜覓情
肅尋無
無處

域息
城消
巡郎
柝無
擊多

側弋聽
在被膩
已終吐
郎鴻胸
情孤曲

嚀行驚
叮郊情
余中春
聽夢情
諦使飲
毋毋欲

榻見應
牙何不
象將見
牙之呼
夜輾卧
轉

揢市編
臥閒跡
出与忌
欲場躕
儂廣康

卒士
戍山
多郎
城彼
郎叩

人把家
邏郎娘
巡把入
離身偎
纏反倚

子女眾城郎
歌山深羊鈴
躋荒落今毋
繾綣方懞郎

What is that coming up
        from the wilderness,
    Like a column of smoke,
Perfumed with myrrh and frankincence,
    With all the fragrant powders
        of the merchant?

Behold, it is the litter of Solomon!
About it are sixty mighty men
    Of the mighty men of Israel,

All girt with swords
    And expert in war,
Each with his sword at his thigh,
    Against alarms by night.

King Solomon made himself a palanquin
    From the wood of Lebanon.

He made its posts of silver,
    Its back of gold, its seat of purple;
It was lovingly wrought within
    By the daughters of Jerusalem.

Go forth, O daughters of Zion,
    And behold King Solomon,
With the crown with which
        his mother crowned him
    On the day of his wedding,
    On the day of the gladness of his heart.

何物臄外来　厥狀類煙烓
没藥与乳香　金粉共薰照
奧来諸珍品　敗運賴商賈

所羅門皇興　周遭六十士
以色列之特　英勇無倫比
個乚帶其邪　善戰又輕死
腰間縣寶刀　夜來防不軌

所羅門乚塹榖
利巴嫩木其身

其底黃金　其柱純銀
坐墊深獄色　喬皇若九春
邮城众俠女　獻霙作文菌

錫安諸美女　迸英所羅門
頭上載金冠　瞻姿盖龍軒
心花方怒敉　熱烈慶新婚
王母為加晃　日角耀朝暾

133

CHAPTER FOUR

Behold, you are beautiful, my love,
Behold, you are beautiful!
Your eyes are doves
    Behind your veil.
Your hair is like a flock of goats,
    Moving down the slopes of Gilead.

Your teeth are like a flock of shorn ewes
    That have come up from the washing,
All of which bear twins,
    And not one among them is bereaved.

Your lips are like a scarlet thread,
    And your mouth is lovely.
Your cheeks are like halves
      of a pomegranate
    Behind your veil.

Your neck is like the tower of David,
    Built for an arsenal,
Whereon hang a thousand bucklers,
    All of them shields of warriors.

Your two breasts are like two fawns,
    Twins of a gazelle,
    That feed among the lilies.

第四首

美至爾
美至彌

面蓋花羅帕
明眸似鴿子
駿若山羊群
基列坡下逶

貝齒如群羭
綿毛新受薙
一一哺乳無
洗淨方出脆

唇猶紅線圈
繡口呼蘭苣
顳顬石榴片
蒙在綸巾裏

秀項匹高臺
大衛藏棘矢
上千縣盾牌
衛盾千勇士

乳峯殊溫潤
母麕孿生麛
嬉戲百合叢
齧食菜與莧

Until the day breathes

    And the shadows flee,

I will hie me to the mountain of myrrh

    And the hill of frankincense.

You are all fair, my love;

    There is no flaw in you.

Come with me from Lebanon, my bride;

    Come with me from Lebanon.

Depart from the peak of Ama'na,

    From the peak of Senir and Hermon,

From the dens of lions,

    From the mountains of leopards.

You have ravished my heart,

        my sister, my bride,

    You have ravished my heart

        with a glance of your eyes,

    With one jewel of your necklace.

How sweet is your love,

        my sister, my bride!

    How much better is your love than wine,

    And the fragrance of your oils than any spice!

清風起天際　　煙歛雲霧霽
余投沒藥岫　　乳香崗上棲

我愛洵全美　　瑤璧皎無瑕

同出利巴嫩

我新婦　　　　我嬌娃
同出利巴嫩　　安步以當車
越波阿瑪那　　又陟示尼碚
一凌黑門頂　　窺探獅子窩
遠迍豹子巇　　萬劫眼底過

我妹子　　　　我新婦
奪我心　　　　不用手
明眸轉秋波　　項鍊承華首

我妹子　　　　我新婦
愛情甘如飴　　香醇勝美酒
哪嚏氣絕倫　　椒衢難比耦

Your lips distil nectar, my bride;

> Honey and milk are under your tongue;

> The scent of your garments is like

> > the scent of Lebanon.

A garden locked is my sister, my bride,

> A garden locked, a fountain sealed.

Your shoots are an orchard of pomegranates

> With all choicest fruits,

> Henna with nard,

Nard and saffron, calamus and cinnamon,

> With all trees of frankincense,

Myrrh and aloes,

> With all chief spices —

A garden fountain, a well of living water,

> And flowing streams from Lebanon

Awake, O north wind,

> And come, O south wind!

Blow upon my garden,

> Let its fragrance be wafted abroad.

Let my beloved come to his garden,

> And eat its choicest fruits.

朱唇溢甘露，蜂房如繡口，
舌凝蜜與酥，餘韻遍且久，
衣如利巴嫩，郁烈世希香。

爾乃封鎖園，我妹我新婦，
脈脈溢靈源，禁錮之苑園。

園中多佳果，妙品有石榴，
鳳仙苞吐豔，哪噠樹含苞。

藝哪噠与蕃紅花兮，雜菖蒲桂樹以為儔。
滋乳香沒藥於斯畹，萃異卉與沈香為一疇。

憶乃活水井，園中自悠悠，
爾源絕清冽，利巴嫩下流。

北風兮興起，南風兮吹来，
吹進兮園內，香馥盡發新，
良人其臨格，鮮果勝新醅。

CHAPTER FIVE

I come to my garden, my sister, my bride,
I gather my myrrh with my spice,
I eat my honeycomb with my honey,
I drink my wine with my milk.

Eat, O friends and drink:
    Drink deeply, O lovers!

I slept, but my heart was awake.
Hark! my beloved is knocking.
"Open to me, my sister, my love,
    My dove, my perfect one;
For my head is wet with dew,
    My locks with the drops of the night."

I had put off my garment,
    How could I put it on?
I had bathed my feet,
    How could I soil them?

第五首

新婦　　　　　　　　　　武妹子
入園圃　　　　　　　　　余今入園圃

香与醴飲，芳袖懷酣，　　藥蜜沒蜂房，探食其蜂，言言。
聚乳哺，請詠。　　　　　歡讌兮，情侶兮，讀。

猶低珍人，心聲所完，　　上門，榻叩子，臥人妹，置身良。
竈訴，新津。　　　　　　子繡曲，鳩啟已，我妹，爲我。

寢柔我，我首余其色，　　啟局，聽我，我駿。
身發，再復染。

上濁，身塵，　　　　　　服呈，晚雙，濃懷已已。
披染，曷盍。　　　　　　脫濯，已已。

141

My beloved put his hand to the latch,
     And my heart was thrilled within me.

I arose to open to my beloved,
     And my hands dripped with myrrh,
My fingers with liquid myrrh,
     Upon the handles of the bolt.

I opened to my beloved,
     But my beloved had turned and gone.
My soul failed me when he spoke.
I sought him, but found him not;
     I called him, but he gave no answer.

The watchmen found me,
     As they went about in the city;
They beat me, they wounded me,
     They took away my mantle,
     Those watchmen of the walls.

I adjure you, O daughters of Jerusalem,
     If you find my beloved,
That you tell him
     I am sick with love.

What is your beloved more than another beloved,
     O fairest among women?
What is your beloved more than another beloved,
     That you thus adjure us?

良人探手入門隙
儂一瞥見動心魂

門淳淪　人開而　良漬為　良手捷　為兩水

逅舍駕　迎守不見　空神也　戶神也　啟儂貞

池陂　繞儂　城也　析奪　擊復

思痴　所情　懨病　遇正　徜餞

殊與姝　何所世　究予絕　愛君爾　所諸咨

赴汁上　衣藥捷　振沒木　爾滿濡　遂指沾

去時音　身語同　轉低無　人彼之　良方呼

卒傷　邏受　遇至　門儂　出毆

兮達　女轉　眾代　城祈　邨千

士節嘔　吉風叮　他高相　比有乃　若抑故

My beloved is all radiant and ruddy,
    Distinguished among ten thousand.

His head is the finest gold;
    His locks are wavy,
    Black as a raven.

His eyes are like doves
    Beside springs of water,
Bathed in milk,
    Fitly set.

His cheeks are like beds of spices,
    Yielding fragrance.
His lips are lilies,
    Disttilling liquid myrrh.

His arms are rounded gold,
    Set with jewels.
His body is ivory work,
    Encrusted with sapphires.

His legs are alabaster columns,
    Set upon bases of gold.
His appearance is like Lebanon,
    Choice as the cedars.

His speech is most sweet,
    And he is altogether desirable.
This is my beloved
      and this is my friend,
    O daughters of Jerusalem.

所愛勝萬人　面白双顋朱
其首若精金　髮鬂密麗鬈
色澤玄以黑　玄冪似慈烏
眼如溪邊鴿　閞對靈源立
記置眞適宜　沐浴以乳汁
酺猶香花畦　其氣郁且烈
唇乃百合苞　沒藥液外溲
手臂黃金管　嵌玉白勝雪
象牙雕作身　鑲石藍而潔
脛寄精金座　宛然膏柱樹
貌肖利巴嫩　秀於石香柏
口吻甜且美　全然更愛慕
郇城諸女子　敢煩已關注
斯是偄良人　相知已有素

CHAPTER SIX

Whither has your beloved gone,
    O fairest among women?
Whither has your beloved turned,
    That we may seek him with you?

My beloved has gone down to his garden,
    To the beds of spices,
To pasture his flock in the gardens,
    And to gather lilies.
I am my beloved's
      and my beloved is mine;
    He pastures his flock
      among the lilies.

You are beautiful as Tirzah, my love,
    Comely as Jerusalem,
    Terrible as an army with banners.

Turn away your eyes from me,
    For they disturb me. —
Your hair is like a flock of goats,
    Moving down the slopes of Gilead.

Your teeth are like a flock of ewes,
    That have come up from the washing,
All of them bear twins,
    Not one among them is bereaved.

隔途 何歧 注嘆 愛免 所庶

畔羝人淪 花與良隱 香輸我中 彼放我合 進牧我百

撒灂拔 得壯挺 似殊何 美景旗 爾旌旌

奪逸 所下 為列 魄基 魂基

出殘 水夭 自遭 淨一 洗無

姝覓 色爾 絕助 爾儕 咨我

團花戎羝 團合乎與 下百屬輸 愛摘人放 所採良牧

兮城旅 愛郇一 鍾若振 所麗武 余秀威

余羊 視夏 莫如 瞬黑 轉鬃

輸生 群學 若得 齒匕 牙個

Your cheeks are like halves of a pomegranate
  Behind your veil.

There are sixty queens
    and eighty concubines,
  And maidens without number.

My dove, my perfect one, is only one,
  The darling of her mother,
  Flawless to her that bore her.
The maidens saw her and called her happy;
    The queens and concubines also, and they praised her.

"Who is this that looks forth like the dawn,
    Fair as the moon, bright as the sun,
    Terrible as an army with banners?"

I went down to the nut orchard,
    To look at the blossoms of the valley,
To see whether the vines had budded,
    Whether the pomegranates were in bloom.

石榴分兩瓣　　帕中顙顱骨

六十后　　　　八十妃
並無數裹子

我雛鴿　　　　我完人
此一人而已

乃母所獨生　　鍾愛無倫比
眾女慕高華　　后妃咸稱美

外觀若黎明　　秀麗奪月霸
試問斯何人　　皓如朝曉白
威武展旌旗　　雄師待奪翩

園桃核下懷　　谷中察蕃蔚
葡萄萌芽否　　石榴開苔未

Before I was aware, my fancy set me

    In a chariot beside my prince.

Return, return, O Shu'lammite,

    Return, return, that we may look upon you.

Why should you look upon the Shu'lammite,

    As upon a dance before two armies?

依稀螢蝶夢　　飄然迷眾芳
不覺登王車　　六龍顯華貴

　回轉与　　　田轉與
　　書拉密女兒
　回轉與　　　回轉与
　　顧瞻爾令儀

覩書拉密女　　爾曹欲何為
宛觀瑪哈念　　軍中之舞姿

"依稀螢蝶夢"一段意譯,可參閱白話譯文之說明。

151

CHAPTER SEVEN

How graceful are your feet in sandals,

    O queenly maiden!

Your rounded thighs are like jewels,

    The work of a master hand.

Your navel is a rounded bowl

    That never lacks mixed wine.

Your belly is a heap of wheat,

    Encircled with lilies.

Your two breasts are like two fawns,

    Twins of a gazelle.

Your neck is like an ivory tower.

Your eyes are pools in Heshbon,

    By the gate of Bath-rab'bim.

Your nose is like a tower of Lebanon,

    Overlooking Damascus.

第 七 首

王女歟　　　　　王女歟
　兩足著鞋步上蓮
　圓腿光潤勝羨玉
　自經哲匠所磨研

膣同圓杯子　　酒醴滿其室
厥腰小麥堆　　百合繞戌畦

乳房溫且輭　　母鹿孿生麑

項似象牙座　　眼若清水池
　靜豪巴拉濱門外
　隱然希寶本之陸

鼻梁直而端　　如利巴嫩塔
徬彿有所慕　　朝大馬士磕

"膣同圓杯子"係據 THE INTERPRETER'S BIBLE, VOLUME 5, 135面之註釋者。

153

Your head crowns you like Carmel,

And your flowing locks are like purple;

A king is held captive in the tresses.

How fair and pleasant you are,

O loved one, delectable maiden!

You are stately as a palm tree,

And your breasts are like its clusters.

I say I will climb the palm tree

And lay hold of its branches.

Oh, may your breasts be like

clusters of the vine,

And the scent of your breath like apples,

And your kisses like the best wine

That goes down smoothly,

Gliding over lips and teeth.

I am my beloved's,

And his desire is for me.

頭猶逶密山
髮絡披至肩
綠雲深紫色
玉心為紆纆

燦爛灼人
何令其身落
棕髴

余余而所愛慕
亭亭玉立碩果
王碩

枝垂香芳
樹下果蕾
棕櫚雙蘋蕾
握之氣齒
緊景吹唇

撥葡萄酒暢
攀葡萄美舒
欲似匹極
今乳吻咽
余瀰香下

我慕我良人　彼亦不相忘

Come, my beloved,
    Let us go forth into the fields,
    And lodge in the villages;

Let us go out early to the vineyards,
    And see whether the vines have budded,
Whether the grape blossoms have opened
    And the pomegranates are in bloom
There I will give you my love.

The mandrakes give forth fragrance,
    And over our doors are all choice. fruits,
New as well as old,
    Which I have laid up for you,
        O my beloved.

藏莊棚萌榮，馨盈誠
偕村葡已春，清以衷
子於葡芽學，播充濃
与宿觀否蕊，一限表
願投同是吐人以愛情，處户藉

人野圃花橘，良子　華果子
良田圃開石，莘佳君
我下入園已安，我將饗農　怒諸與
兮乚晨否見，陀舊獻
來行明是能，蔓新故

157

CHAPTER EIGHT

O that you were like a brother to me,

That nursed at my mother's breast!

If I met you outside, I would kiss you,

And none would despise me.

I would lead you and bring you

Into the house of my mother,

And into the chamber of her that conceived me.

I would give you spiced wine to drink,

The juice of my pomegranates.

O that his left hand were under my head,

And that his right hand embraced me!

I adjure you, O daughters of Jerusalem,

That you stir not up nor awaken love

Until it please.

Who is that coming up from the wilderness,

Leaning upon her beloved?

Under the apple tree I awakened you.

There your mother was in travail with you,

There she who bore you was in travail.

第 八 首

子真儂手邑，哺乳恩同深。
在外間邂逅，吻子不自禁。
孰敢相輕蔑，有子繫儂心。

攜子入母宅，内室相規箴。

饗子以香酒，石榴汁共斟。
左手為儂枕，右擻背至襟。

郎城諸女子，讀聽余叮嚀。
千祈須仔細，勿令夢中驚。
郎儂方繾綣，欲飽春情。

伊誰野地想，弱如楊柳枝。
託身寄君子，搖曳自生咨。

苐果樹底下者，余喚醒細君。
令堂在此卿，為爾千力勤。
掬育愛卿，於斯耕耘。

Set me as a seal upon your heart,
　　As a seal upon your arm;

For love is strong as death,
　　Jealousy is cruel as the grave.

Its flashes are flashes of fire,
　　A most vehement flame.

Many waters cannot quench love,
　　Neither can floods drown it.
If a man offered for love
　　All the wealth of his house,
　　It would be utterly scorned.

We have a little sister,
　　And she has no breasts.
What shall we do for our sister,
　　On the day when she is spoken for?

If she is a wall,
　　We will build upon her a battlement of silver;
But if she is a door,
　　We will enclose her with boards of cedar.

I was a wall,
　　And my breasts were like towers;
Then I was in his eyes
　　As one who brings peace.

置余爾心頭
銘鐫作印璽
或在腕臂間
鑴刻成戳記

愛情強固死凶境
嫉恨兇殘陰府地

淋燄是雷鞭
炭上熱且熾

眾水淹也不息滅
洪流沖也益縱恣
傾家以求之　必為所戲棄

吾曹有一妹
乳峯未豐滿
苟人欲議婚
難言郤与竅

為築銀堆堞
倘彼是城牆
為封香柏板
倘彼是門防

儂曾作城壁
兩乳是樓臺
儂在彼眼裏
曾帶平安來

Solomon had a vineyard at Ba'al-ha'mon;

He let out the vineyard to keepers;

Each one was to bring for its fruit

A thousand pieces of silver.

My vineyard, my very own, is for myself;

You, O Solomon, may have the thousand,

And the keepers of the fruit two hundred.

O you who dwell in the gardens,

My companions are listening for your voice;

Let me hear it.

Make haste, my beloved,

And be like a gazelle

Or a young stag

Upon the mountains of spices.

請看所羅門
置一葡萄園
交園丁經營
在巴拉哈門
為園中果寶
人須付千元

余之葡萄園
區區此一廛
佳果為我熟
嬌花亦嫣然
敬陳所羅門
君自蔭一千
園丁培壅苦
應得兩百負

寄語園中子
德音希勤宣
伙伴樂諦聽
幸不我棄捐

深願我良人
迅速勿稽延
猶如羚与麚
山上偎芳荃

此次"人須付千元"，應作"每人付千元"。茲依歌底斯譯法，請參白話譯文。

余今欲攀援　緊握棕樹枝
爾乳似葡萄　纍纍雙下垂

置余爾心頭　銘鏤作印誌
或在腕臂間　鐫刻成戳記

附　錄

（一）

怎樣在中國建立基督教文化

一九四七年八月廿二日講於鼓浪嶼福音堂靑年禮拜。

讀雅歌三章1——4；馬太十三章：52；

這個問題的重要性，是教會中有識之士所公認的；過去教會中的袞袞名流曾經熱烈地討論過，現在把他們所遺漏，而卻是最重要的幾點，申述如下（雖然因爲時間的關係，不能詳細的闡述，但大體已具），以就正於教會中諸先進，希望他們有以見教。

剛才主席已將所要念的聖經念過了。今天所着重的是第四

節，不過現在先把其他三節簡略地檢討一下：

第一節請大家注意三點：

一、夜間　白天我們過着尋常的生活；在萬籟俱寂的晚上，可以讓我們過着一種超越尋常的生活。很多作家在晚上完成他的偉大作品。元朝趙孟頫的一首詩，前兩句說：「明明秋夜月，流光照羅帷」。這樣的一剎那，便把人生的意味提到更高深的地方去了。又有兩句：「良人遠行役，萬里歸無期」。這是描寫閨中的思婦，想念到她的良人到很遠的地方去（或者是經商，或者是從軍），不知道甚麼時候回來。

又夜間是黑暗的，可怕的，有狼吟虎嘯。現在是天快亮的時候，所以也特別來得黑暗。

二、床上　床上是歇息的地方。

三、尋找我心所愛的，可比方尋找眞理。舊說這是描寫以色列絕世佳人阿比煞想念她所心愛的牧羊人的詩歌。阿比煞是選來事奉大衛晚年的。及所羅門卽位，雖然有成千的妃嬪，卻不會滿足他的心意；因爲「我的完全人只有一個。」因爲這女子美麗得像一朵百合花。主耶穌說；當所羅門極榮耀的時候，他的衣裳比不上百合花的一朵。因爲他不能用他豐富的物質，金錢，地位，權力獲得眞的愛情（要知道世上的奸商，市儈，有毒病的人，都用他們不乾淨的手去拿過錢）；「始知絕代佳人意，卽有千秋國士風」！我們也要像她這樣的追求眞理。

當達摩大師到中國來時，有個青年人去找他，看見他兩手合十，兩眼緊閉，坐在大石壁的前面：那青年不敢驚動他，那天過去了，第二天和晚上也過去了，大師還是坐着。這位青年忍不住了，拔出他的劍，把自己的一隻手臂斫掉了；因爲很

167

痛，便唉喲地叫了起來。達摩大師才張開他的眼睛，用憐憫的聲調對他說：「青年人啊！你要甚麼？」「我的心很痛苦。」是的，我們現在的心中有痛苦，更要追求。

第二節請大家注意兩點：一，我要起來　基督叫我們要負起十字架來跟從他。所以基督徒也要能夠吃苦；經上說；「我要起來」，從什麼地方起來呢？是從象牙之榻出來的。

二、城中　街市上和寬闊的地方。這些地方都是找不到真理的，卻是充滿罪惡的地方。據統計倫敦三百五十人中有一人中梅毒；紐約二百五十人中有一個；上海一百五十人中有一個。我曾經到過戲院，想要把心中的愁悶遣掉。但是裏面的人，有的吃瓜子，有人抽香煙，有的說些很難聽的話，不但不能消愁，反而使我心靈更加沉重起來！有人說：外國的戲院就不是這樣。然而那些影片，到底有多少看的價值呢？曾經去看過名片「出水芙蓉」，除了那些色彩和滑稽的動作以外；再也找不出有甚麼藝術的價值。我們看了這種片子，只表示我們的趣味是低級的而已！

第三節巡邏看守的人　這些是傳道者，他們的任務和那些「防備夜間有驚慌」的勇士大同小異。

第四節要注意三點：一、找到心所愛的　我們找神，神亦在等候我們；「求就得着，尋找就遇見」。

二、不容他走　「道也者，不可須臾離也」「不隨流失去」。

三、入我母親的家　母親可比喻做我們的祖國。要讓基督教文化在中國生根。基督教已經在中國傳了四次；第一次在唐朝，傳了一百多年，有寺院四百多所，現在徒留穹碑子子！第二次在元朝，第三次在明朝；後來都失傳了。一百多年前馬禮

遜傳教到中國來是第四次的了；這次會不會失傳還是個疑問。

佛教傳到中國來，也曾碰到「三武之厄」；但使佛教能夠繼續傳下去的，不是他們能夠戰勝逼迫，而是有建立一種佛教的文化。儒家雖然闢佛，然而儒家的學理太膚淺了，不能滿足中國士大夫的求知慾，所以都向佛氏投降了。像唐代文豪韓愈，有衛道文章的「原道訓」，有作政治性的制止的「諫迎佛骨表」，但後來也向佛氏投降了(這是儒家不肯承認的)。唐宋以來學術思潮的主流是佛教，直到現在中國最大的書店——商務印書館，本來跟廣學會有血緣的關係，現在裏面刊行很多佛教的書籍，卻沒有一本屬於基督教的，除了最近吳經熊博士譯的聖詠譯義以外。

現在我們要知道中國的需要正是在建立基督教文化。可分三點來說：

（一）醫治中國國民的劣根性　中國現在很多的思想家批評中國國民的劣根性是貧，病，愚，弱，私（但是他們沒有提出醫治的方法）；徐寶謙先生再加上一項說，中國人沒有「正義感」。歷史上漢有王莽之亂，晉有五胡亂華，唐有安史之亂，宋有靖康之恥，明有流寇之亂，要找像張巡，顏杲卿，文天祥，史可法之流，真是鳳毛麟角，卻滿是魏忠賢的義子。所以有人故意表彰費宮人，沈雲英這些婦人女子的愛國舉動，要叫那些「社稷之臣」羞愧。

我們翻開西洋史抑福克思的殉道錄一看，主後三百年間的信徒，和路得馬丁之後的新教徒殉道的情形，未免相形見拙！從司提反起，所有的使徒除了約翰而外，沒有一個善終的；然而約翰也被放逐到拔摩海島上。

169

陳獨秀有一句話說：「巴不得把基督的血注射到每個中國人的血管裏。我們要把基督豐富的生命表彰出來，使中國人有正義感」（革命先革心）。

（二）樹立思想及道德的權威　我常用一個有趣的比喻，現在講給大家聽：五四以來，胡適之，陳獨秀，錢玄同，吳虞等先進，倡議打倒孔家店，全國靑年靡然從風，有的丟石頭，有的打夥計，弄得孔二先生沒有辦法，只好收場，宣告停業。但孔家店在兩千多年來，可算是一間「無限公司」：中國人要買什麼便有甚麼。此後卻沒有人會開這麼大規模的店鋪，只有舊貨攤。胡適之，陳獨秀，錢玄同，魯迅，郭沫若，梁漱冥，馮友蘭都是。或向外國杜威，羅素，馬克思，恩格斯等販點東西來，或是向古時的孔，老，莊，佛等販點來，擺在街旁道左，等着顧客們的賞光，有的甚至招搖撞騙，買空賣空。所以道德權威倒了，思想錯雜紛歧：良可浩嘆！『千里而一士，是比肩而立焉；百世而一聖，若隨踵而至焉」（戰國策）。中國今日有誰再來做孔子第二，而爲人師表，使這段歷史不至空虛呢？

我們要來用另外一套邏輯學去研究基督教的哲理（像羅馬書一至十一章是說我們在基督裏與神發生的關係，十二章至末了，是說我們在基督裏和人發生的關係），成爲一部方法嚴密，規模洪博的哲理，來代替儒，道，佛的東西，來領導中國人的思想，而樹立道德的權威，不要讓瞎子再領路。『凡文士受教作天國門徒，就像家主，從他庫裏拿出新舊的東西來』（馬太十三章五十二節）。

（三）建立基督教文學　魯迅有篇文章叫「鴨的喜劇」，

寫到俄國盲目詩人愛羅先珂來北平，說：『寂寞呀，寂寞！沙漠一般的寂寞。』是的，中國近代沒有偉大的作家。雖然有人把魯迅稱爲中國的高爾基，但有一次一個作家叫魏猛克，畫一張魯迅與高爾基的漫畫，把高爾基畫得又高又大，把魯迅畫得又小又矮。也沒有偉大的作品。鄭振鐸，傅東華編文學的時候，曾用這樣的問題問讀者：『中國爲什麼沒有偉大的作品』？現在的中國，經過百年來的壓迫，三四十年來的革命，八年來的抗戰，是何等偉大的時代？爲甚麼沒有產生代表這一代的作品呢？尤其是新詩，更是可憐。以前有一位先生告訴我說：他花了六毛錢去買一部卞之琳的詩集。那集子的前頭，錄了唐朝李商隱的兩句詩：『鶯啼如有淚，爲濕最高花』。這兩句在唐朝算不了什麼，然而他花了六毛錢，只買到這兩句！

『中國新文學之成功，小品文之成功也』。這是林語堂人間世發刊詞的兩句話。郭沫若在「懷知堂」一文曾說：現在中國的作家，可以在國際上跟人家分庭抗禮的只有周作人。如今周氏不幸失足，誰來繼承他做灼照千秋的偉業呢？

聖經是世界文學的淵源，我們要來根據它建立一種基督教文學，來代替有毒的文學，以及雜牌的文學。

最後：請大家看腓立比四章十三節做結束；『我靠着那加給我力量的，凡事都能作。』希望大家靠主的能力，向前邁進！

——錄自閩南聖會報第六十卷第八期

（二）

王福民：閩南故名牧王師蒼公之叔子。歷任惠安私立培仁小學校長，福建省立龍溪中學文女史教員，青年之友編輯，廈門私立毓德女中行政秘書；菲律賓濱馬尼剌新聞日報編輯，編輯部顧問；聖公會、嘉南、靈惠、中正等校高中文史教員。一九五七年經自由中國教育部審定爲大學講師。一九六一年秋遊歐，參加漢學會議於漢堡大學，探倫敦大學英博物館之敦煌稿本，參與學術研討會。一九六三年秋返菲，任中正學院副教授、教授，學報編輯。一九七二年出長納卯中華中學。一九七五年獲中華學術院授給榮譽學位。一九七九年任東方日報總編輯，世界日報編輯。一九八四年移民美國，卜居南加州，曾在中華歸主神學院講授中國哲學史、文化史等課。譯著已出版者：語文雙譯雅歌、靈犀詩論、書學抉原。其他學術論著、散文、時論、古文、舊詩，亦將陸續付梓。

朱一雄：國立廈門大學中國文學系學士，菲律賓聖多瑪大學美術學士、碩士。擅版畫及油畫。其金屬鏤刻獲全菲第八屆美展第一榮譽獎；木刻版畫獲東南亞美展版畫

第二獎，菲全國第十二屆美術版畫首獎。初任菲美術協會理事，現代畫會副會長。著有"美術論文集"等書。繼任萊西安學院、現代畫廊、美術協會講師。一九六八年與夫人莊昭順及女兒四人移居美國。先在新英格蘭四家州立大學巡迴講師。旋應維眞尼亞州之華盛頓與李將軍大學之聘，充駐校畫家並美術、美術史教授。一九八九年退休，獲校董會尊爲終身榮譽教授。

丁　星：菲律濱基督教大學哲學教授、協和神學院專題研究諮詢顧問，聖經公會輔導委員會翻譯組組員。主要著作：英譯中國古代短篇故事，鍾如戟與老子玄學思想之比較（歐柏林文學碩士論文），莊子之玄學——其倫理及宗教價值之評衡（牛津哲學博士論文）。一九七五年獲中華學術院授與榮譽學位。一九七七年應東海大學之聘，將代梅貽寶老教授之課，一年後將赴紐西蘭大學任哲學教授。不幸罹不治疾，遽返天家，齎志以歿，令人痛惜！

WHO'S WHO

of

THE SONG OF SONGS

IN ENGLISH AND CHINESE TRANSLATIONS

ROBERT GORDIS is a professor of the Jewish Theological Seminary of America.

The scholars who labored in the Old Testament Committee of the Revised Standard Version are:

Dean Luther A. Weigle, Yale

Prof. Millar Burrows, Yale

Pres. F. C. Eiselen, Garrett

Prof. George Dahl, Yale

Prof. J. P. Hyatt, Vanderbilt

Dean Fleming James, U. of the South

Prof. H. G. May, Oberlin

Prof. Jas. Muilenburg, Pacific School of Religion

Pres. J. R. Sampey, Southern Bapt. Seminary

Dean W. L. Sperry, Harvard

Prof. C. C. Torrey, Yale

Prof. Wm. R. Taylor, U. of Toronto

Prof. James Moffatt, U. T. S.

Prof. W. F. Albright, Johns Hopkins

Pres. A. R. Gordon, United T. College, Montreal

Prof. W. A. Irwin, Chicago

Prof. J. A. Montgomery, U. of Penn.

Prof. H. M. Orlinksy, Jewish Institute of Rel. N. Y.

Prof. Kyle M. Yates, Southern Bapt. Theol. Sem.

Prof. J. A. Bewer, U. T. S.

Prof. J. M. P. Smith, Chicago

Prof. Leroy Waterman, U. of Michigan

ONG HOK BEN is the third son of a well-known pastor in the southern part of Fookien province, the late Rev. Wang Shih Ts'ang also known as Ong Shi Ts'ung. He was one of the recipients of the Timothy Lee Essay Award. Principal of P'ei-jen Elementary School in Huei-an; a teacher in Chinese literature and history at Lung-chi Public Middle School, and the secretary of the Yu-te Girls Middle School, he was an Elder of the Chinese United Evangelical Church of the Philippines, editor of Fookien Times, instructor in Chinese literature and history at ST. Stephen, Hope Christian and Chiang Kai Shek High School. In 1957, the Ministry of Education in free China granted him to be a qualified college instructor. He visited his brother Mr. Wang Yu Min in Hamburg, Germany in 1961 and participated in the International Sinological Conference there. He was ableto see historical sites in Europe. In England he called on Sinologist in London and Cambridge and was able to view the Dun Huang manuscript at the British Museum. He returned to the Philippines to be a professor at Chiang Kai Shek College in Chinese classics in 1963-72. The China Acadamy of free China conferred upon him the honorary Doctorate Degree IN Philosophy in 1975. Later he was Editor in Chief of the Tong Fang Daily News and Editor of World News. In Los Angeles he lectured in History of Chinese Philosiphy at Chinese for Christ Theological Seminary and retired in 1987.

I-Hsiung Ju was born in Kiangyin, Kiangsu, China, in 1923. He graduated from the National University of Amoy in 1947 and received his A.B. degree in Chinese Art and Literature. Because of the war in China, he went to the Philippines to teach and at the same time to continue his studies. He graduated from the University of Santo Tomas in Manila and received his B.F.A. and M.A. in History.

He has been considered as one of the few Chinese artists able to blend two worlds of style, technique, and idiom to produce a unique form of painting which is both modern and traditionally Oriental. According to Prof. Ju, "a Chinese artist is not only a painter, but also a poet and a philosopher."

A prize winner in graphic art, oil painting, and Nanga works in various countries, a writer and lecturer on art, he has held many one-man shows in Australia, Canada, China, England, Hong Kong, Japan, the Philippines, and the United States. He is the author of many books and numerous papers on Chinese art.

As an Artist-in-Residence and Professor of Art at Washington and Lee University, he was selected Professor of the Year for 1971 by the Ring-tum Phi, the Washington and Lee University newspaper, and was awarded the Best Art Educator of the Year for 1974 by the Chinese National Writers and Artists, Association in Taipei, Taiwan, the Republic of China.

Prof. Ju retired from Washington and Lee Univ-

176

ersity in 1989 and was honored by the board as Professor Emeritus, He is the founder of the Art Farm Gallery which has been conducting Chinese painting workshops. Beginning in 1990, the workshops will continue along with his correspondence courses.

SIMON TING has been a professor of philosophy at the Philippines Christian College since 1950. He is also a research consultant of the Union Theological Seminary of the Philippines and a member of the translation commitee of the advisory council of the Philippine Bible House. He is the author of various literary and religious essays published in the local newspapers. Some of his major works are: Selected Short Stories from Chinese Classical Literature (1946), A Comparative Study of Mysticism in Rufus Jones and Lao Tzu (M.A. thesis, Oberlin, 1950), The Mysticism of Chuang Tzu (D. Phil. thesis, Oxforg, 1958). He was confered with an honory Doctorate degree in philosophy by China Acadamy of free China in 1975. In 1977 he recieved two invitations to teach at Tonghai University and New-Zealand University of New Zealand, but unfotunately he could not carry out this teaching job, he passed away due to cancer.

哭丁星博士四律

王福民

一、讀破東西萬卷書　　　　放洋涉曠又經虛
　　聖言在抱謙恒益　　　　柔弱爲懷智若愚
　　執教期匡天下溺　　　　論文待起泰西儒
　　秋墳血碧千年恨　　　　惠子空誇富五車

二、動心忍性閱飢寒　　　　十架在肩豈畏難
　　鄰火殃來書稿燬（註一）　聘函雙至燭心殘（註二）
　　彌留腸斷金蘭友　　　　大去輪空長者班
　　悵望千秋誰照灼　　　　屋樑落月淚闌干

三、大道亡羊哭路歧　　　　生民渾噩竟誰依
　　英賢未遇塡溝壑（註三）　志士若狂痛黍離（註四）
　　大器晚成難受職（註五）　韜光養晦憤臨池（註六）
　　抱樽信誓爲歸計（註七）　獨恨春蠶未吐絲

四、瓠落莫容任棄捐　　　　鷦鳩只解笑鵬摶
　　井黽作主情殷厚　　　　海客依人味索然
　　梟獍效廉遮腐鼠　　　　鸜鵒消渴乏甘泉
　　午窗蝶夢終成幻　　　　漫道指窮火不傳

註一：一九六〇年僑區大火博士住宅成灰燼，存稿及大量珍貴藏書，
　　　均被焚。

註二：繼東海大學之後，紐西蘭大學將聘博士於一九七八年秋起，
　　　任該校哲學系主任。

註三：家長兄王新民教授，自幼發憤為學，及壯，未嘗稍輟；中英
　　　文、文、史、地、哲諸學，均具深厚之根柢，一九六〇年死
　　　於廈門禾山勞改營，年僅五十。

註四：王德明兄，西南聯大研究助教，中法大學、雲南師範學院講
　　　師，返菲後得菲大史學碩士，一九九〇年獲語言學博士。

註五：勝進博士曾在弘一法師指導之下，著「韓偓」一書，因國變，
　　　在開明書店所排之版，竟遭銷毀。一九七五年得英國Read-
　　　ing University生物學博士。某大學以其屬退休年齡，不予
　　　聘用。一九八四年「韓偓」在臺出版。

註六：藏珠盦早歲來菲，傳道，辦學，編報，乃赴美從商，後轉往
　　　西德。暇時揮毫作字，其分書抗衡伊秉綬，其行草，當代尠
　　　有其匹。

註七：余廿餘年前與藏珠盦，勝進居士遊侖禮沓，遇雨，避入
　　　Bayview Hotel小酌，口占一絕：
　　　霧下長堤失釣磯　　　　　抱樽但欲願無違
　　　聊看隔座佳人笑　　　　　風雨兼天未許歸

179

後　記

　　本書由嘗試性的譯作，變成一本書，經過十三年才得和世人相見，的確是

上主的鴻恩。一九四八年，我開始根據King James英文本翻雅歌一至四首爲五古，是我從事譯作的開始。從一九四九至一九五八，這十年間，在報上發表過的譯作約六七十萬言，十份之九是宗教性的。這部書的後四首五古，和白話譯作全部，是我這十年譯事最後的果實。所以這本書實在和我第一階段的翻譯工作相終始，於我生命史上，是很值得紀念的一件事。

　　這本書的成功問世，除得了丁星教授（M. Simon Ting）的敦促，幫助謄寫、打字、校閱外，還蒙家仲兄王鏞民先生資助印刷費，畫家朱一雄兄替我插圖，設計封面，書家劉鐵庵醫師代書序言的字，白話譯文有蔡景惠小姐代爲打字，方美同學代爲謄寫；又承盧增緒教授之助，得在國內再版，使我非常的感激，特地在此向他們誌謝。